FILMMAKERS SERIES
edited by
ANTHONY SLIDE

Some Cutting Remarks

Seventy Years a Film Editor

Ralph E. Winters

Edited by Laurie Holz

Scarecrow Filmmakers Series, No. 88

The Scarecrow Press, Inc.
Lanham, Maryland, and London
2001

SCARECROW PRESS, INC.

Published in the United States of America
by Scarecrow Press, Inc.
4720 Boston Way, Lanham, Maryland 20706
www.scarecrowpress.com

4 Pleydell Gardens, Folkestone
Kent CT20 2DN, England

British Library Cataloguing-in-Publication Information Available

Library of Congress Cataloging-in-Publication Data

Winters, Ralph E.
  Some cutting remarks : seventy years a film editor / Ralph E. Winters.
    p. cm. – (Scarecrow filmmakers series ; no. 8)
  Includes index.
  ISBN 0-8108-4024-3 (alk. paper)
  I. Title. II. Filmmakers series ; no. 88

  TR849.W56 A3 2001
  778.5'35'092–dc21
  [B]

                                                        2001031346

♾ ™The paper used in this publication meets the minimum requirements of
American National Standard for Information Sciences—Permanence of Paper for
Printed Library Materials, ANSI/NISO Z39.48–1992.
Manufactured in the United States of America.

DEDICATION

To all the great MGM film editors who went before me. Who beat me. Who tortured me. Who taught me. Who were constantly bothered and pestered by me. Who burned their knowledge into me.

Never have I known a more dedicated group of people than these superb practitioners of our craft. Wonderful people all.

CONTENTS

PREFACE

At a recent party, my host introduced me to another of his guests, saying, "Meet Ralph Winters, a close friend and a two-time Academy Award winner."

"Really," said the guest, very impressed. "And for what did you win these awards?"

"For film editing," I proudly answered.

"Oh," he said. He didn't seem too impressed anymore. A weird look appeared on his face as he strolled away. I felt like calling after him, "Gee, sir, I'm sorry. I didn't mean to offend you."

A film editor is the person who puts a bunch of film together and tries to make an entity out of a lot of isolated scenes or angles. Despite the general public's lack of awareness of the job, it is often said that the editor makes or breaks a picture. I really don't think that is quite true. Well, maybe, in a few, very isolated cases.

Many directors—though not all—believe they are great editors. Usually, they are not. This breed of director sometimes accepts less than the best because they don't know what the best is. Sometimes neither the director nor the producer knows too much about the wonderful art of film editing. When this is the case, the picture can suffer. However, a good film editor may save the day.

I always liked to think that every picture I ever edited was a better picture because I edited it.

"You have just about every honor an editor can have," my dear friend Larry Mirisch said to me. I have been basking in his comment and reflecting on my career. If you'd like to hear about some of the funny and strange things that happened to me, and learn a bit about editing along the way, please read on.

ACKNOWLEDGMENTS

With boundless gratitude, I happily acknowledge the help of T. Gene Hatcher. He is my friend and one of the most erudite men I have ever known. Without his wonderful help I would surely be lost in a sea of words. . . . Thank you, Gene.

Also, I must acknowledge Laurie Holz, my editor. It was a happy day for me when she accepted the assignment. Among her many great contributions was the title of this book. Her help and patience were immeasurable. . . . Thank you, Laurie.

Chapter 1

When I think of the people who have really had a strong influence in my career, I would put Ralph Winters right up there. He has the great qualities of a director, a sense of leadership and knowing. If Ralph said, "I've got an idea I want to try [on *Kotch*]," I would always let him. And . . . as a human being, he is one of the most outstanding people I have ever met.

—Jack Lemmon, June 14, 1995

In 1924, Marcus Loew, the owner of Metro Pictures, bought Goldwyn Pictures, creating Metro-Goldwyn Studios. Loew then bought Louis B. Mayer Productions and hired Mayer to head the new studio. Within a few weeks of the merger, Loew agreed to add Mayer's surname to the title, and—out of these mergers—a new film company was born: *Metro-Goldwyn-Mayer*.

A wonderful alliteration that was to become famous.

Within two years of the merger, MGM was flowering. Its slogan was "More Stars Than There Are in Heaven." It was true. Almost every big star in the industry was eventually under contract to MGM: Norma Shearer, Clark Gable, Greta Garbo, Robert Taylor, Elizabeth Taylor, Spencer Tracy, James Stewart, Joan Crawford, Judy Garland, Robert Montgomery, and many more.

At its height, MGM employed twenty-five hundred people and had a weekly payroll of a million dollars. It had ninety writers under contract, and so many directors they had to have their own building. Everything that was necessary for the making of a movie, MGM had on its Culver City lot: its own wardrobe department, filled with countless costumes of every period, a

1

construction department, a machine shop, a paint shop, a carpentry shop, an art department, a casting department, a building half the size of an airplane hangar to hold props, and on and on.

An idea could walk in the front gate and go out the back gate a whole and complete movie.

So how did the son of a poor Jewish tailor come into this great industry just a moment in time before *Metro-Goldwyn-Mayer* and the rest of the motion picture industry flowered?

To answer that question requires a bit of our family history. There was my father Sam, my mother Millie, my sister Silvia, and me, little Ralphie. We were a modest Jewish family living in the back of my father's tailor shop in Philadelphia. We were at one time or another living in Toronto, Montreal, and Philadelphia. My father was a chubby, fair-complexioned man who never lost his Brooklyn accent. He was a marvelous tailor, a ladies tailor, and a real perfectionist. And though I often managed to get into trouble with him, I loved him very much.

Whenever I was a bad boy, Dad made me get under his working table. I had to just sit there, watching his legs move back and forth as he cut patterns and then the cloth for ladies' suits. This always cost me time away from my toy fire engines. Sometimes, it was pretty late before I could get them back to the station. Since I intended to become a fireman when I grew up, I had to be very careful with all this complicated equipment.

At age nine, I became ill and the doctors told my mother that I should be taken to a warm climate. My mother had a sister who had moved to San Bernardino, California, with a sick husband, so that is where we wound up in the winter of 1918, right after the end of World War I. During the next few months, as I started to regain my health, I joined the YMCA and learned to swim and play pool. The next year, Dad bought a brand new car, on time—a 1920 Ford. It was the first model with a self-starter. No more cranking by hand. Boy, was he excited! I helped him build a garage for it in the back yard. We seemed to be slowly coming up in the world.

Dad was a very meticulous man and he insisted that I be the same way. Each and every day when I came home from school, it was my job to clean the yellow spokes on the wheels of the Ford before I went into the house to do my homework. Each day when Dad came home from work, he also went into the garage on an inspection tour before he came into the house. After a few raps on the knuckles, I became a very good spoke cleaner. Years later, when I got my own car, he insisted on giving my wheels a close examination. Thank goodness I passed inspection. I couldn't get away from him. God bless him!

But Dad couldn't hack it in San Berdoo, and in 1925, we moved to Los

Angeles. When we left, he was three thousand dollars in debt to the Bank of Italy. He got a job designing ladies' suits for fifty bucks a week. As time went on, I was amazed to see that he paid back every cent to the Bank of Italy.

My mother's uncle, Jake Levy, played pinochle with a guy by the name of Jerry Mayer, who happened to be the brother of Louis B. Mayer. Now these two guys—Jerry and Louie—also happened to be mad at one another. Jerry was opening a fancy tailoring shop on the second floor of some fancy building on Hollywood Boulevard. In spite of the anger that existed between the two brothers, Louie furnished the new tailoring shop with all the rococo furniture, props, and drapes from *The Merry Widow* picture. Uncle Jake got Jerry and my Dad together and Dad went to work for Jerry in the fancy tailoring shop. Everything was going along fine until the following Passover when Jerry and Louis were at a seder together and made up. Jerry gave up the fancy tailoring shop and went to work at MGM. And bingo! Dad was brought to MGM to work in their wardrobe department. Lucky MGM!

Dad worked hand in glove with Adrian, the world-famous costume designer who was under contract to MGM, and who designed exclusively for all the stars—men and women alike. Adrian would hand my father a sketch and just by looking at it, Dad could figure out exactly how much cloth was needed to make a gown or costume. (Whenever chamois was needed for a Western costume, somehow there would always be enough left over for washing a car!) Then Dad would set about making the costume. Once the process got underway, Adrian would come in to look and make suggestions.

My father was always quiet, respectful, and capable, and everyone called him "Sammie." Everyone except Greta Garbo, who called him "Saum." At that time, Garbo was the most glamorous, mysterious, and aloof movie star of all filmdom and her name a household word around the world. Though Garbo guarded her privacy in the extreme, she was always relaxed and jovial when she came to the wardrobe for a fitting. In fact, Garbo was very fond of Dad and loved to banter with him.

Garbo would put on her costume in the privacy of her dressing room, then come out into the fitting room where Dad was waiting with his pins and needles. My father was a very shy guy, but a tailor has to use his hands when doing a fitting, and Dad could tell that she was naked under her costume. As he molded the cloth to her body, he would turn beet red. Then Garbo would tease him, asking in her very sultry voice, "What's the matter, Saum?"

The same year Dad went to work for MGM, our family was blessed with twin boys, and they were a handful. At seventeen, I was chief diaper washer and dryer. Every day after high school I would wash and hang out at least fifty diapers to dry. I kept after the yellow spokes, too.

By the time I was eighteen, Dad could occasionally get me a job as an extra. I was an extra in *The Trail of '98,* a silent movie starring Dolores Del Rio and Ralph Forbes. I played a sailor in a picture called *Valencia* starring Mae Murray. It was worth playing hooky from high school; the pay was three bucks a day—not too shabby. Hey, you could get a lot of mileage out of three bucks in 1927. A guy could take his girl out to dinner on three bucks. I always gave my mother two dollars and kept a buck for spending money.

The following year, when I turned eighteen and was ready to graduate high school, my family could not afford to send me to college. The only way I could have attended college was to work my way through, and I didn't think I could get the best education that way. Besides, the picture business was already in my blood. By now, the Winters family was living in Culver City.

The wardrobe department where my dad worked was just across the studio street from the editorial department's building. On the other side of our building was a big stage. The path between our building and the stage was known as "cutting alley."

Dad decided that I should have a job in the editorial department on my way to being made the head of the studio. He acquainted himself with the head of editorial, Danny Gray, a tough little Irishman who also hailed from New York and spoke Brooklynese—"film" was pronounced "fillum." Danny was a short fellow with auburn hair and a rather large, crooked nose that was etched with hills and dales, but I was in complete awe of this imposing figure of a man. Dad made Danny a couple of suits and *voilà,* I had a job.

At first, the job was not at the studio but in the laboratory where the film was developed. The lab was Consolidated Film Industries on Melrose Avenue in Hollywood, and we lived in Culver City, ten miles away. My shift was from eight o'clock in the evening until four o'clock in the morning. Eight o'clock in the evening? Yep! It was scary. During the first week, I thumbed a ride to work and thumbed a ride home every morning. Then Dad bought a 1923 Chevy, with no top and a cone clutch for fifty bucks. He probably found it in some cave. Every time I let the clutch out, the car jumped about twenty feet. But it got me back and forth.

I was assigned to work in the drying room. Picture three long glass boxes, each about four feet in width, fifteen feet long, standing from ceiling to floor. The wet film enters the box through a slot at one end, goes over rollers, which carry the film through the box while hot air is blown through the box, and comes out the other end dry. It arrives on reels that hold a thousand feet, which is the industry standard. All three machines going at the same time. When the reel fills up, you better be there to break the film and catch the loose end coming out of the machine, and start a new reel. These three machines never stopped and they used to really keep me hopping. I felt like Charlie Chaplin working in the factory in *Modern Times*.

I got one day off a week. From my salary of eighteen dollars a week, I gave my mother fifteen and kept three. That job only lasted three months, thank goodness. I was laid off when work became slow due to the tax season. Every year, every piece of picture negative left in the state of California after March 15th was taxed. It was therefore incumbent on picture studios to ship all the negatives of unfinished and finished pictures out of the state by that date because the tax was quite heavy. On an ordinary run-of-the mill movie that cost $500,000 dollars to make, the tax could be as much as $25,000. (Later, much later, Governor Ronald Reagan abolished this tax. What a boon to the motion picture industry.)

I was hoping and praying to get a job at MGM, and in April 1928, Danny Gray hired me as an assistant editor at the studio. Hallelujah!

Now little Ralphie began to swim in the vast ocean that was MGM.

Chapter 2

I didn't know a sprocket hole on a piece of film from a hole in the ground, but I was getting twenty-five bucks a week. Hey, I was a king!

Best of all, I got to see my dad. Because film was flammable, I had to step out of the cutting room whenever I wanted to smoke. I would run over to the wardrobe department for a quick few minutes to chat with my father. I will cherish those wonderful moments forever.

On his first day at work, Ralphie was going to get his first major lesson, and I can honestly say that it burned into him like a dogie getting branded.

I was made the assistant editor on a silent picture entitled *Four Walls,* a prison story starring Joan Crawford and John Gilbert. My editor was Harry Reynolds, a wiry little guy with a sharp nose and a lean look. He had small, brown, flinty eyes and straight brown hair.

One of my jobs was to carry the film from the cutting room to the projection room and back to the cutting room. For some reason, film editors never carried film. This was an unwritten law—you know, like only seniors in high school could wear corduroy pants. It looked pretty funny to see some poor assistant editor staggering along with a load of film in his arms while an editor walked along beside him, empty-handed.

On the morning of that first day, we were showing the rushes, or "dailies" as they are called now, to the producer of the movie, a white-haired gentleman by the name of Harry Rapf. Mr. Rapf became upset because he thought Joan Crawford's gown was cut too low—too décolleté. In today's world, the picture would get a PG rating, but this was the era of Will Hays, the censor czar of moviedom, and censorship was very tough. Mr. Rapf wanted the scene retaken.

"Throw this stuff out," Rapf said. "It's no good."

Being Mr. Eager Beaver, I grabbed the two reels of film, ran out of the projection booth, and rushed back to the cutting room. Our cutting room was on the second floor of the cutting room building. Outside, at the end of a narrow balcony, was a giant, empty trash can into which I threw the film. At four o'clock in the afternoon, Harry Reynolds turned to me and said "Take the rushes back to the projection room. Mr. Mayer is anxious to see them."

Louis B. Mayer, the head of the biggest movie studio in the world, wanted to see the rushes! Suddenly, I felt like a giant mass of Jell-O. "I threw them out like Mr. Rapf told us to do," I answered, my voice quivering.

My boss went white. "Find them!" he snarled.

I took off like a wounded deer. I clattered down the narrow balcony. I tore the lid off the ash can, which was about three-quarters full of all kinds of junk, and dove into the can headfirst. I dug through sawdust and other bits of trash to the very bottom, and there, thank God, were my dirty but precious rushes. I blew most of the dirt off, and triumphantly carried the two reels to the projection room.

Unbeknownst to me, positive film was never physically thrown away. Although a new print could be made from the negative, which was stored in a vault, every piece of positive film—good or bad—was kept in the cutting room until the picture was finished.

Harry Reynolds certainly should have killed me and I think he wanted to. He was a mean bastard and a hard taskmaster who kept me on edge constantly. He was always very tense and uptight. He was really tough. Later in my career, as I looked back, I realized that he was the hardest man I ever worked for. Maybe that was good.

Once he told me to find a piece of a scene that he needed. This piece came from the middle of a scene that had been put in and taken out of the picture a couple times already. I hunted high and low through dozens of scenes. No luck. At the end of the day, he said, "When I come in tomorrow morning, I want to see that piece of film on my bench."

I stayed at the studio all night, going through every scrap of film in the cutting room. It was lost! Panic!! It was now 6 am and time was running out on me.

Down to the negative vaults I raced to see Jerry, a woman with thick muscular arms and slicked-back, dark brown hair. She was a great lady and a good friend. Jerry was in charge of a small vault that took care of the negatives of all the movies during their first week of shooting before they went into their permanent places in the main negative vaults. Jerry located the negative of the scene, ran it over to the lab, and had a print made for me.

I placed the film, a whole new print of the scene Reynolds wanted, on his bench. Of course, when he came to work that morning, he figured out exactly what had happened. But he just looked at me and never said a word.

Sometimes, when the director overruled the editor, the assistant editor got caught in the middle. William Nigh, the director of *Four Walls,* walked into the cutting room one day when Reynolds was out. Nigh, a long, slim drink of water and a nice guy, wanted a change made in the picture. He asked me to make the cut, but I was scared to death. I wound the reel down to the place he was talking about and he made the cut. Cut? Hell, in the old days, the editor or the director took the film between thumb and forefinger and just snapped it. Only sissies used scissors. Sometimes the "snap" would rip through two or three frames of film. Then, when the film was spliced, those torn frames would be lost. Later, when sound came in, the film had to be cut very carefully. The picture and the soundtrack had to be kept to the same length in order to hold sync. In the *real* old days—when "moving pictures" first started—they never even made positive prints. They never had editors. They just cut the negative to what length they thought was correct and made release prints right from the negative.

When Reynolds came back to the cutting room, he gave me hell for allowing Nigh to touch the film.

During the next few months, I behaved pretty well except for the following incident. One day, I wandered into the cutting room next door and saw an assistant editor eliminating every other frame from a scene. If you take a strip of film, eliminate every other frame and then run it on the screen, the action will go twice as fast. Boy, I thought that was a swell idea. I knew just the scene in our picture that needed the same treatment.

I rushed back to my cutting room and was about halfway through the surgery when Mr. Reynolds walked in. He took one look at what I was doing and ran out of the room. I had a feeling in the pit of my stomach that I was in deep trouble—or deep something else. He was back a few minutes later with Danny Gray, the head of the department.

"What do you think you're doing?" he demanded.

I wondered myself. The audacity and nerve of what I had done washed over me like buckets of cold water. I felt like such a fool. I was absolutely tongue-tied and so frightened he could not get a word out of me. I'll never know why I wasn't fired. Probably because Danny Gray was an angel. That poor piece of film was so mutilated, they had to make a new print.

When you're on a movie lot, anything can happen. One day, while walking on the lot, I saw this gorgeous woman who seemed to be looking for something on the ground. It was Joan Crawford. Joan Crawford was the most beautiful woman I had ever laid my eyes on. She had just become engaged to marry Douglas Fairbanks Jr. I asked her if anything was the matter.

"I dropped the diamond ring Doug just gave me," she said. "And if I lose it, he'll kill me."

I fell to my knees like a plummet and helped her search for the ring until we found it. She thanked me profusely.

These were still the days of silent movies. After a picture was cut together, titles were written and spliced into the film. You could change a whole story using different titles. At MGM, there was a group of writers who worked with the directors and producers on the titles, which were essential to the picture.

On the day of a sneak preview, there was always a batch of new titles to be cut into the picture. These usually came from the lab late in the day because producers and title writers worked on new ideas up to the last moment before the preview deadline. The editor would put the new titles into the picture using paper clips, and then the reels would be turned over to the assistant editors who in turn would take out the paper clips and splice the title and picture together. In those days, splices were made by hand. The assistant editor scraped the emulsion off at the frame line with a razor blade, applied film cement to the scraped-off part and laid the next piece of film on to the scraped-off film. It was pretty primitive. All the assistants to all the editors were called in to help splice these titles into the picture, and I was one of those called in to splice. Actually, the quality of an assistant was judged on how good his splices were and how fast he could make them.

Once in a while, we assistants would have a splicing contest to see who among us could make the fastest splice. There was this one guy who could make two and a half splices a minute. No one could beat him. My best speed was about two splices in a minute and a half.

Anyway, that's when I first met a fellow named Sam Zimbalist. He was considered one of the top editors at MGM, and I was assigned to help splice titles into one of his rush pictures before a preview. Little did I realize that one day he would come into my life in an important way.

Meanwhile, the year went by and I managed to avoid getting into any more trouble. Nineteen twenty-nine was rushing up on us. Sound was coming in and I was becoming a top assistant editor. No more foolishness. I got a five dollar raise and I never even asked for it. Thirty bucks a week. Wow!

Dad helped me trade in the jumping old Chevy and I bought a 1929 Willys Knight roadster, blue and gold, with spare tires in wells on each of the front fenders. As soon as I could save enough, Dad ordered some Arrow shirts for me—silk broadcloth, five bucks a shirt. Wholesale. I asked him to order a "quarter of a dozen." Not "three." Oh no! A quarter of a dozen. It sounded better. Big man on campus!

One day, Louis B. Mayer called a meeting of the editorial department. Gee! It wasn't often that the big boss came around. We convened in the open space outside "cutting alley" in front of the Washington Street bathroom.

"We're going to make 'talkies,'" he announced to the thirty-five editors and assistants gathered before him.

This was an exciting proposition, but then he asked, "How are you going to cut them?"

Danny Gray got up and said, "Mr. Mayer, if you can shoot them, we can cut them." Danny had a lot of nerve, as no one in the entire editorial department had a clue as to how the job could be done. At the time, we did our editing on a Moviola. A Moviola is a piece of machinery that you can view a piece of film through. Picture a shoe box that holds a shoe, size thirteen EEE, standing on end, slightly tilted forward with a magnifying glass at the top. Inside the box is a motor driven by a foot pedal, much like the one that would run a sewing machine. It would be small enough to sit on one's desk.

Now to make a sound Moviola: the silent Moviola was set on a little table the size of a typewriter stand. Next to the Moviola, they set a contraption that the sound track runs through. It was interlocked with the picture Moviola so they would run together and stay synchronized.

During this time we had the use of just one sound Moviola for the entire cutting department. I can still see the editors lined up waiting for their turn to use it. Meanwhile, the machine shop was working feverishly to convert other silent Moviolas to sound. The whole department worked on the challenge every night for many weeks. Trial and error, trial and error. But the job finally did get done. All the major studios, including MGM, made their own sound equipment. Everything was bastardized. It took years before any kind of standard equipment was in use.

It was now October 1929. The stock market crashed and heads were rolling like kingpins. I was lucky, and so was my dad—we didn't get laid off. In fact, my dad, who was now the head of the tailoring shop, bought a giant, spruce-green Willys Knight sedan. Thank God it didn't have yellow spokes. He always kept his cars looking as beautiful as the day he bought them. Whenever Dad bought a new car, all his tailors always lined up to see which one would be lucky enough to buy his old one.

I was still stuck with Harry Reynolds and people were still debating the fate of "talkies." Harry was cutting our first "talkie" assignment, a sound picture for Tod Browning, *The Thirteenth Chair,* starring Conrad Nagel. I heard these two visionaries talking one day when they were leaning over the balcony railing, having a smoke. Browning said to Harry, "Sound is just a fad. It will never last. Why, your ears can't even take the sound of paper crackling." Hmmmm.

Harry was cutting a picture that E. Mason Hopper was directing, *Their Own Desire*. Irving Thalberg, whose name graces the coveted award that is given out yearly by the Academy of Motion Picture Arts and Sciences, was producing, and two of the biggest names in Hollywood, Norma Shearer and Robert Montgomery, had the leading roles.

One day, Thalberg decided to run the picture when Harry was sick at home. Thalberg wanted to view the film anyway and asked that I run it with him. I found myself in the projection room with Thalberg, Norma Shearer, general manager Eddie Mannix, lyricist Lorenz Hart, and a couple of other biggies. I was as nervous as a cat. While we ran the picture, Thalberg gave me cutting notes. I was expecting the tough kind of treatment I got from Harry the Hammer. Instead, every once in a while, Thalberg stopped the run, and very considerately asked me if I was keeping up okay with his notes. What a doll that man was. And I made all the cutting changes by myself, too! Pretty good for only two years in the cutting room.

Let me take a moment to explain "cuts." The word is used in two ways: first, as a verb, when you "cut" into a piece of film with a scissors, for example. But if an editor has four scenes, say, a long shot, a medium shot, and two close-ups, he has four different shots. Now when he cuts them into the picture, he will have four different scenes in sequence. Then the word "cut" becomes a noun and each scene is referred to as a "cut." When cutting is discussed, the director might suggest, "put a cut of the close-up into this sequence." Or, he might say, "take out the cut of the long shot."

Finally, after two years with Reynolds, I was reassigned. I felt like I was being released from Devil's Island. Would you believe Harry screamed bloody murder about losing me? He told me that I was the best assistant he ever had.

He did another nice thing. When *Four Walls* finished shooting and was in a "first cut," the shooting crew, as was the custom, was invited in to see the picture. Just before we started to run the picture, Reynolds sent me out of the projection room to get something he had forgotten. I was gone about three minutes and assumed I would miss the start of the movie. But when I came back, everyone was sitting there, waiting for me. Reynolds held up the start of the screening so that I would not miss the beginning of the picture. The man had a heart after all.

It's 1930. I'm now twenty-one years of age. I can vote! I started to play golf. God only knows where I got the makeshift set of clubs I played with.

My dad came to my rescue and bought me a set of Spaulding Sweetspot Irons, the first irons made with steel shafts. I still have the putter. I cadged a set of derelict woods, and Jack Conway, the famous director, gave me a driver.

MGM had a golf tournament every year and, naturally, I entered it. All the movie stars and the companies MGM did business with contributed prizes. Duncan Renaldo, the star of *Trader Horn,* donated a pair of Congolian goat horns. These consisted of two short horns, about six inches in length, jutting out from a piece of stained wood. I was resplendent in a white polo shirt and beautiful white linen knickers made by, who else, my dad. I shot a miserable score of 140, which still earned me a spot in the prize lottery. I guess the three other guys in my foursome were not too good.

About three hundred guys gathered on the lawn in front of the wardrobe department to see who got the prizes. As each prize was brought up, a name was drawn from a hat. When the goat horns were brought up, the breath caught in three hundred throats. Three hundred hearts stood still. When my name was drawn as the winner of the goat horns, a mighty roar of relief rose from the three hundred throats. It was an apt prize for a guy who shot 140.

I don't know whatever happened to those horns. I wish I had them now.

After two years as an assistant editor, I was making thirty-five bucks a week. I was promoted to cutting "trailers"—coming attractions—but the new job did not come with a raise. I was very unhappy about that, but I swallowed my unhappiness and kept quiet, as this was a definite promotion.

Although I was still a member of the editorial department, Frank Whitbeck, the head of the advertising department, was now my boss. He was big, robust, and tall with white hair, hands like two hams, and a deep booming voice. He slipped me fifteen dollars a week out of his expense account. Gee! What a swell guy. Thoughtful and generous. Fifty bucks a week. I had an assistant, too. No more throwing film in the ash can. No more eliminating every other frame.

We would get a list of the scenes needed for the trailer from the New York office. Then we would go to the editor of the particular picture with the list of scenes and collect the film that was needed. These were outtakes usually, and if there were no outtakes, then we would have the original takes duplicated in order to have negative for every scene used in the trailer. Then we would ship the material to New York where the trailer was completed. Eventually, it became more expeditious to complete the trailers at the Culver City studios under Whitbeck's supervision. This was a good job for me and gave me a chance to watch the editors, to be in their cutting rooms, and to study the way they worked.

Once in a while, an editor would let me cut a simple sequence for his movie. I would grab these opportunities like a dog after a bone. I begged editors for "outtakes" to practice with and would come in Sundays on my own time to work on them.

In 1932, Universal Picture studios was doing sensational business with *Frankenstein.* Irving Thalberg wanted MGM to make an even more horrible horror movie. It came up with *Freaks,* a movie so horrible that even the people on the lot wouldn't look at it. Every known misshapen creature in the country was brought to MGM. The lot was full of these strange, sideshow characters walking and crawling around while the picture was being made.

My family and I lived within walking distance of the studio and one night I left the studio around six o'clock. It was already dark. I crossed Washington Boulevard and headed up the street. Suddenly, I heard a low moaning sound. As I walked on, the moaning became louder. I was scared. I hesitated. I started to cross the next intersection, and, as I approached the curb, I came upon a little man standing in the street next to the curb. He could not have been more than three feet tall. He was now moaning a little louder. I bent down and asked, "What's the matter?"

"I have terrible arthritis," he replied, in a high-pitched voice, "and I can't get up onto the sidewalk." The curb was about a foot and a half high and this poor little guy just could not manage it. I picked him up and set him on the sidewalk. "God bless you, son. God bless you," he said in his high-pitched voice. I continued walking home. I felt good.

One Saturday in July 1934, a friend called me to go to the beach. I demurred, saying I was too tired. But he insisted, saying he had a date with a cute girl and some of her friends down at the beach. I gave in, and of course, I got very interested in one of the girls. Her name was Estelle Joy Iseman. Her nickname was Teddy. I liked her. She was slim and weighed about 99 pounds. She was a redhead and a ball of fire. I fell in love with her. Seven months later, we were married. She was 20, I was 25. I was making thirty-five bucks a week. Hey! I was a man of responsibility.

Chapter 3

Anyway, the 1930s were slipping by. MGM got bigger and better, and I continued to get better. I sopped up everything I could lay my hands and eyes on. I cut a couple of "Our Gang" comedies. Danny Gray even sent me over to Hal Roach Studios one time to cut a Laurel and Hardy episode, as they needed some editorial help. I was becoming the jack-of-all-trades around the editorial department. Once in a while, I would be handed a sequence from a feature to cut without supervision, just to help an editor who might be overloaded with work. Eager to get a feature picture of my own to cut, I received these chances with open arms.

MGM had a "short subject" department, which was a great learning ground. Young directors like Fred Zinnemann, Jules Dassin, and Roy Rowland, and young producers like Richard Goldstone and Buddy Adler came out of the shorts department. Buddy Adler eventually became the head of creative affairs for 20th Century-Fox. I was very happy and delighted when I finally made it to this level.

While there, I cut a short called *They All Come Out,* a good four-reeler about the U.S. Treasury Department. A full reel holds about ten minutes of film. When MGM discovered they had no release for a four-reeler, they had more story written and made *They All Come Out* into a feature-length movie. Seven reels. It was a fluke, but my first real credit as an editor. However, I was still working in the shorts department. I cut a short for Fred Zinnemann about the tsetse fly. The story takes place in Africa. From that moment on, Freddie and I called each other "Bwana." And then later, much later, I cut his first feature-length movie, *Kid Glove Killer.*

It was 1939, the year *The Wizard of Oz* was in production. One day

15

when I went to the wardrobe department to pay Dad a visit, he had a bunch of tin laid out on his cutting table. "I thought you were a tailor, Dad. I see you are really a tinsmith."

"I'm making the tin suit for Jack Haley to wear in *Wizard,*" he told me. "The prop department was afraid to tackle it, so I got the job." What a guy. And he did a hell of a good job, too.

Ray Bolger, who played the Scarecrow, spoke fluent Yiddish. Dad had lots of fun bantering with him while making the scarecrow suit.

By chance, I learned that an assistant editor, a friend of mine, had gotten a script of his own and was about to be promoted to editor. Crazed with anger that I had been overlooked, I ran up to Danny Gray's office and past his secretaries like a whippet. There was about a four-inch rise at the entrance to his office. I truly don't remember tripping but the next thing I know, I was flat on my back at the front of Danny's desk, looking up at the ceiling, and Danny was peering at me over the edge of his desk. I must have interrupted his reading of the *Daily Racing Form.* All the fight went out of me. I slowly got up and weakly pled my case. Danny told me not to worry, as I would soon be getting a shot at my own movie.

World War II had started in Europe, but I was oblivious of everything except my hunger for a chance to cut my own feature picture. I was given a 2A classification—exempt because I was in the entertainment business and cutting training shorts for the Army and Navy. I was still schlepping along and my family was growing. One lovely little daughter. One brand new daughter. And still another daughter coming in the distant future.

I had now been an assistant editor and jack-of-all trades around the editorial department for thirteen years. Would I ever get my break?

One day, the door to my cutting room opened. My boss, Danny Gray, looked in. In his hand was a script. I stared. Was this it? He threw the script onto my bench. He didn't say a word. He shut the door.

I grabbed at it. It was a new script. Oh, my God!! I had my own picture at last. This was not a fluke! I rushed up to Danny's office, and this time I didn't trip. I hugged him. I kissed him. I flew over to the wardrobe department. I hugged and kissed my dad. "Dad! Dad! I finally made it. I'm a cutter. We're both cutters. Tailors are cutters. You're a cutter. So am I. You cut cloth. I cut film. Isn't that great?" I ran back to my cutting room and opened up the script. *Mr. and Mrs. North,* starring Gracie Allen, to be produced by Irving Asher and directed by Robert Sinclair. I was certain MGM was about to produce the greatest picture of all time!

I was now thirty-two years old. Thirteen years had passed since my first day as a green assistant. The first dailies came in. I took the film in my hand.

My own film, my very own. I started to edit. Ah, but I was tentative, and very nervous. I'd put a sequence together, take it to the projection room, look at it, and begin to worry that it wasn't any good. I would get one of the older editors to take a look with me for any ideas he might have. Then I would recut, trying to improve.

Enter Margaret Booth, one of the great film editors of all time. She was small in stature and slim. Well, more like thin. Nooo, she was downright skinny. She was fair of complexion, yet she was not a blonde. Margaret looked like a lady who should have been born early in the nineteenth century. She was now forty-three years old. This lady was to have a tremendous and far-reaching effect on my career.

She had worked for Mayer when he had his own studios on the north side of Los Angeles, and when the merger had taken place, Mayer had brought Booth with him to MGM. She was twenty-six years old. A film editor who had come from being a negative cutter (negative cutting was just a mechanical procedure) to being a positive film editor. When Thalberg had come to MGM, Margaret had edited all of his personally produced pictures: *Mutiny on the Bounty, Camille, Romeo and Juliet,* and others. There were other women editors, damn good ones too, such as Blanche Sewell, who cut *The Wizard of Oz, Boom Town,* and other great movies. Anne Bauchens was Cecil B. DeMille's editor, and Barbara McLean, Irene Morra, Anne Coates, and Dede Allen were well respected.

When Thalberg had died, Mayer had made Margaret Booth *supervising* editor of all pictures at MGM. She was given her own projection room, where she viewed all rushes and dailies of every picture made at the studio. She was unique—she only had to answer to Mayer. But she wielded her power like a giant shillelagh. Producers and directors feared her. When she liked the dailies, she would write a nice note to the producer or director praising the film. When she did not like the film, she would run up to Mayer's office to complain.

MGM had a unit system that worked like this: Mayer made some of his very knowledgeable men—Sam Katz, J. J. Cohn, Arthur Freed, and others—executive producers. Each of these executive producers had five or six producers under him and each of these executive producers would be responsible for his unit's output. It was a good way to work when the studio was making forty-five to fifty pictures a year.

Arthur Freed, Pandro Berman, Sam Zimbalist. When you were assigned to be an editor for one of these producers, Margaret did not supervise your work. However, she looked at all film shot for MGM and reported to Mr. Mayer.

Every morning, I brought my work to Margaret, as she was the supervising editor on *Mr. and Mrs. North*. And every morning she ate me for breakfast for the entire movie. She picked on about 85 percent of my work. Time and again, I was sent back to the cutting room to correct a match or to fix a cut. Once, she asked one of the older editors to make a match for me. I wasn't very happy about that one. A "match" is cutting two scenes together, that is, when cutting from one angle to another angle, the action of the actors must be the same, so that the action doesn't jump to the eye. Some matches can be very tricky, but there is always, almost always, a clever way to cheat so that the eye of the viewer is not disturbed.

I was worn out by the end of this pip-squeak of a movie. One day, I passed Margaret and Frank Sullivan (an editor whose work I loved) in the hallway outside of the projection rooms. I heard her say, "I wish they were all like you, Frank." I vowed that one day she would praise my work.

In December 1941, the United States went to war. Most of the younger fellows were conscripted into the Army, but though I was given a 2A exemption, I had my own war. My work load was very heavy. Under normal circumstances, it would take six to seven months to cut and finish one picture. But over the next fourteen months, I cut and finished seven feature films.

One thing I tried to learn during this period was to recognize when my own editing was good and when it was bad, when to recut, and when to leave it alone. It took me years to learn how to do this and to be objective about my own editing.

There was a six-week period when I did not get home for dinner once. I think I came out of that era forged in steel.

Well . . . pot metal, anyway.

During the war, directors were allowed to print only one take on any given angle. Silver nitrate that was needed for the manufacture of film was also needed for the war effort. "One-take" printing was tough because sometimes a director needed to print three or four takes in order to cull the best performance from the actors.

However, he could keep a list of the extra takes, and when the picture was finished and cut together, if he felt he could improve performances, he could ask the editor to print up the outtakes. Funnily enough, sometimes the extra takes were not needed after all. Sometimes, the sequences for which the extra takes were printed were taken out of the picture anyway. With less film in the cutting room, the editors' load was lessened.

Today, directors print many takes. Color prints are far more expensive than black and white, and 90 percent of the pictures made today are shot in color. This expense, in my opinion, is obscene. A lot of young directors shoot too many angles and print far too many takes. Some of the reasons for this can be their nervousness, worrying whether they got the scene right or not. Then this mass of film winds up in the cutting room, where the decisions fall to the poor editor, who has to grapple with it.

Smack in the middle of World War II, MGM decided to make *Cry Havoc,* a war drama with an all-female cast. Margaret Sullavan starred in this movie about battlefield nurses. Edwin Knopf, a member of the book-publishing family, produced. He worked my behind off, but I liked him. He was tall, dark, and slim, and a hell of a nice guy. His left hand had been blown off by a grenade right after World War I, but he was not the slightest bit self-conscious about it. He poked me in the chest with his stump whenever he was making a point.

Knopf was a smoker. He would shake a cigarette part way out of the pack with his right hand and bring it to his mouth. Then he would put the pack away with his right hand. He would take a book of matches out of his pocket with his right hand, pin the book against his chest with his left stump, extract a match from the book with his right hand, strike the match while the matchbook was pinned against his chest by his stump, light his cigarette, leave the cigarette in his mouth, take the book of matches away from his chest with his right hand, put them back in his pocket, and continue talking. This whole procedure only took a few seconds, but I was spellbound every time he did it. So much so, that I forgot to listen to what he was saying.

The memorable part of *Cry Havoc* for me was the decision made about how to end the story. Five or six nurses are left in a bunker, and they are about to be captured by Japanese soldiers. We hear the guttural commands of the Japanese ordering the nurses to come up out of the bunker.

We had created two endings. One: when the nurses exit up the stairs, we hear the rat-a-tat-tat of machine-gun fire—nurses killed. Two: when the nurses exit up the stairs—silence, the implication being that the nurses were taken prisoner and raped.

On the afternoon preceding the sneak preview, Danny Gray, my boss, told me that he had been instructed to tell me to put the "happy" ending into the picture. Say what? The United States had now been in the war for almost two years and the moviegoing public was getting sick of war pictures, so maybe the machine gun ending *was* the happy one.

Chapter 4

It was 1944, and sixteen years had passed since I threw away the rushes on my first day at MGM. A lot of water under the bridge. Many of the older editors were gone, fellows whom I had loved and worked with. I was more subdued, quieter, not so rambunctious.

Along comes *Gaslight*. How I happened to land this movie is a mystery. I'm sure Danny Gray had something to do with it, but I was delighted to get the assignment. Big picture, big cast—Charles Boyer, Ingrid Bergman, and Joseph Cotten. This was only my twelfth onscreen credit and I was just getting dry behind the ears, editing-wise.

Margaret Booth was to be the supervising editor. I was getting a bit better after two years of editing and Margaret ate me for lunch only now and again. I was a little nervous because I was going to be working with a couple of heavyweights in the industry: Arthur Hornblow Jr. and George Cukor. Hornblow, the producer, was a very pompous and rather nondescript-looking man of medium height and build, with sparse, graying hair. He was always pulling at his tie and jerking his neck. George Cukor, the director, was a very nice-looking man, and nice, too, also of medium height and build, with black curly hair.

The picture was running way behind schedule. It took eighty shooting days to complete, and the director and the producer were not getting along. I could see that a nice hatred was brewing between these two giants. This did not bode too well for me. In fact, editors are always put in the middle, anyway. To make things more difficult, I had to sit between them in the screening room whenever we were running the picture.

During one run of the picture, a four-foot cut went by on the screen.

A four-foot cut runs for two-and-two-thirds seconds. Hornblow whispered to me, "Trim this shot."

Cukor overheard him and whispered right back, "Add to it."

Well, when I got back to the cutting room and examined the film, I thought it needed neither an "add" nor a "trim." It looked right to me and I decided to leave it alone. The next time we ran the picture and came to this spot in the movie, I nudged Hornblow and whispered, "Okay?" He whispered back, "Great." I nudged Cukor and whispered, "Okay?" He whispered back, "Great."

I was learning some of the fine points of diplomacy.

One day, Hornblow and I were running the picture. His secretary had come along with him. A small, dark, skinny, birdlike person with no personality at all, she was just as pompous as her boss, and I didn't care for her. Her name was Estelle, the same as my wife, which infuriated me even more. We came to a spot in the movie where Boyer and Bergman were doing a heavy dialogue scene while standing in a doorway. I had a two-shot of the actors, and a close-up of each actor. During the progress of the scene, I cut to Bergman's close-up (CU) first and then to Boyer's CU. Hornblow wanted to go to Boyer's CU first and *then* to Bergman's CU.

After explaining to Hornblow why I had cut the scene that way, we continued to run the picture. The next time we ran the picture and came to that spot, Hornblow stopped the picture and said, " I thought you were going to make that change."

I said, "You did not tell me to do it, but I'll be happy to do it your way."

He said, emphatically, "You *do* that!"

Estelle chimed in, "I think Mr. Hornblow's way would be better, too." This poor lady had no way of knowing what cutting was all about. But I made the change.

The next time we ran the picture and that spot came up on the screen, he stopped the projector. "I think that's much better." Estelle said, "Oh yes, Mr. Hornblow, that is much better." I didn't open my mouth. Horny pressed the buzzer and the projectionist started the picture up again.

About a half a minute later, Horny stopped the picture. "Why don't you like it?" he asked like a petulant child. Ahaaa! I had got him. I again explained my reasoning as I had when we first ran the scene. Nicely. Quietly. "Put it back the way it was!" he wailed. I really thought Hornblow decided that he liked it better the first way too. I said nothing. I was not trying to win anything. We went on.

With a chase scene, a fight scene, or any kind of action, when there is movement almost any kind of match will work, especially when there is a lot of movement. Movement attracts the eye. Sound attracts the eye.

But intercutting angles during an emotional scene can sometimes be very tricky. A good director will keep the actors at the right emotional pitch while shooting a delicate scene and while he is shooting various angles of the scene. It's tough. But suppose he works with the actors all morning and finally gets a very good master shot where the actors play the scene beautifully. They laugh and cry and the director is very happy with the result. Now they break for lunch. It's two hours later. A wall had to be taken out and the cameras moved, the set to be relit, etc. They are getting ready to shoot the CUs. Now the actors are not quite at the same level emotionally. They try all afternoon. It's getting late. The director will never get the actors back to the same emotional pitch as they had been before lunch. He prints a couple of takes in disgust. The next day while looking at the dailies with the editor, he says, "Do the best you can with it. Maybe we'll have to reshoot." Now the editor takes the film and studies it, looking for the right spot in the master scene where he can slip into CUs and maintain the emotion without jarring the scene. Well, sometimes he gets lucky and finds a wonderful way to intercut some CUs so that the audience is kept at the proper level of excitement. Sometimes he's not so lucky. Maybe the scene will play without the intercutting of any CUs. Gee, wouldn't that be great! He might get home for dinner.

When cutting a dialogue scene that takes place between two people or among a group of people, the editing must be done very carefully and delicately, because people in the audience react to every little thing the actors do, every movement, every word, every flick of an eyelid. They can easily be distracted by a bad match in the cutting from one entity to another or a bad jump in the sound. When I see a well-cut dialogue scene, then I know I am looking at the work of a good editor.

Whenever a very important scene was ready to be shot, it was customary at MGM to bring the producer down to the set to watch a dress rehearsal. They were ready to shoot the big scene of *Gaslight* and Hornblow was called. On to the set strode the big man, colors flying. The crew waiting with bated breath for the rehearsal to start. I happened to be on the set, and was waiting, also with bated breath. I had a hunch something good was going to happen.

Hornblow walked up to Joseph Cotten and Ingrid Bergman and took hold of Cotten's coat lapel and tugged at it, trying to straighten it out. Here was this important scene in the picture waiting to be shot and Mr. Hornblow was tugging at lapels.

I don't think George Cukor could believe what he saw. Uttering every obscenity in the known world, Cukor flew into a rage, stamped his feet, and told Hornblow to get the hell off the set. Hornblow retreated, his tail between his legs.

After *Gaslight* finished shooting and was cut together, Cukor and Hornblow wanted to retake a couple of scenes. Mr. Louis B. Mayer, L. K. Sydney, Sam Katz, Cukor, Hornblow, and I (I was there for note-taking) met in the screening room and viewed the picture. They decided that they had a fine picture and okayed making the retakes. However, Ingrid Bergman was out of town. As a matter of fact, she was in Sweden. Mr. Mayer, upon hearing this bit of news, rose to his feet. A hush fell. He began to pace up and down. Now all the executives bowed their respective heads and lowered their eyes. Except me. I was not laden with shame and had nothing to hide. Ahh, but I was naïve and unsophisticated.

Now, Mr. Mayer began to blow his stack. When Mr. Mayer got off on one of his tirades, he fixed his eyes on any person in the screening room whom he happened to catch looking at him. He then delivered his whole tirade to that person. And may heaven help the poor bastard if he let his eyes drift off the boss. You guessed it. I was impaled. Nevertheless, I thought it was a real good speech. He went up one back and down another. He never let those guys off the hook. The gist of the oration being, why the hell were the actors released before the picture was set. I'm pretty sure he was enjoying himself. In the end, however, they brought Bergman back and Cukor and Hornblow were allowed to make their retakes.

Mayer was a great executive who built MGM almost single-handedly. He created an empire. He had a canny ability to recognize talent, and he got wonderful talent from every field of entertainment into MGM. He surrounded himself with the best that money could buy. He was never afraid to spend the extra dollar. He always stood ready to help other executives of other studios when they needed help with casting or money. He drove a hard bargain, but he was there for them like a rock.

Whenever one of the other studios made a good picture, the comment was, "This movie has MGM quality." And whenever we sneak-previewed a picture and MGM's lion logo came on the screen, the audience burst into applause. They knew they were going to see something worthwhile even before they knew what the picture was. Quite a tribute.

Any underling in the studio could go up to Mayer's office any time and see the boss. But if you were an executive, you had to make an appointment to see Mr. Mayer. One day when Mayer was walking through the cutting room alley, an assistant editor was coming out of one of the cutting rooms whistling. Mr. Mayer stopped him and asked him why he was whistling. "I'm happy, Mr. Mayer." Mayer looked at him wistfully and said, "I wish I could say the same." Quite a comment from the biggest man in the entertainment world. I thought he was a great guy and much maligned in his later years at MGM, and more so after he left the studio. Shameful!

Louis B. Mayer, in my humble opinion, contributed more to the greatness of the motion picture industry than any other person.

A couple of weeks later, after *Gaslight* was completed, I was walking on the lot when I saw Hornblow and Cukor, two former enemies, walking toward me arm in arm, discussing a new project. Do you think they even said, "Good afternoon, Ralph"? Go figure.

Chapter 5

In 1947, I had another chance to work with Roy Rowland, who was to be the director on *Killer McCoy*. I had just cut two pictures for Roy (he and I got along really well), and he wanted me to cut this movie, too. Sam Zimbalist was to produce. Having worked for Zimbalist when he was an editor made the idea of cutting for him exciting.

Sam was truly a self-made man. Starting in his teens as a projectionist at Metro Pictures in New York, Sam rose through the ranks to become an editor at MGM in Culver City in the late 1920s.

Though his features were somewhat exaggerated, Sam was a nice-looking guy, even handsome in a way. A big strapping fellow, maybe around 6' 2", Sam had a dark complexion and black curly hair that he wore slicked back and loaded with pomade. He was heavy, weighing in at around 225, and his leather heels were fitted with iron taps. Sam walked with a clang and a purpose. He had great charisma and charm.

Sam was now a well-established producer and I looked forward to this assignment. I knew he was tough to work for, but having been an editor, Sam understood the editor's problems. And having worked for him in the silent days, I relished the chance. In fact, I learned more from this man purely by observation than from any other person during my years at MGM; not only about cutting film, but also about many things in life, including a great way to conduct myself, how to work hard and industriously, and to be fair and honest.

He was a heck of a psychologist, too. When I was an assistant and sort of floating around the department, I was assigned to help his assistant editor on the picture *Boom Town,* which Sam was producing. J. J. Cohn was the executive producer whose unit Sam was in. There was a sequence in the picture where Clark Gable and Spencer Tracy put out a fire in one of the oil wells they owned.

27

Cohn kept saying to Sam, "It doesn't have any excitement in it." And Sam kept trying to explain that since the sequence was just an incident in the story and not really a part of the story, it could not have too much excitement in it. "Sam, the sequence needs more suspense," Cohn kept insisting.

Every time we ran the picture, Cohn kept carping to Sam about this moment.

Finally, Sam turned to me and said, "Ralph, make a dupe of the sequence and then recut it for Mr. Cohn." Well, J. J. and I spent a week cutting and recutting. At the end of the week, Mr. C. said, "I think we got it. Let's show it to Sam." Frankly, I couldn't see much difference. Anyhow, Sam came into the screening room and took a look. "Gee," he said. "That looks very good, Joe." "Do you think so, Sam?" "Yeah, Joe. It might just be better. I think I'll exchange it. Put your version into the picture instead of mine." "Just a minute, Sam. Are really sure it's better?" "Well, I think so, Joe. I think we may try your version at a preview." Joe's face paled. "Gosh, Sam, I think we better leave your version in the picture." J. J. bowed his head and closed his eyes. Sam winked at me.

Joe never mentioned the fire sequence again.

Sam was a taskmaster, always demanding but never mean. As tough as he was, I loved working for him because the learning process never stopped. I idolized him and can never say enough wonderful things about this man.

Killer McCoy, a remake of the old Robert Taylor movie *The Crowd Roars,* starred Mickey Rooney as a young smart-aleck boxer. It had five fight sequences in it, and they were tough to work on. In order to save time, the shooting schedule called for them all to be shot at one time, that is, consecutively. When the camera was set up shooting to one corner, for example, everything needed in that corner for all of the five fights would be shot. The two ways to tell the difference between one fight and another were the slates on the beginnings of the scenes, of course, and the different boxers. It took ten shooting days to complete the five fights. There now was a mountain of film to work on, and it took about three weeks to cut all of them.

When Sam and I looked at the first fight after it was cut, he said, "We will now work on this fight until we get it into good shape. We will not work on the next one until we are satisfied with this one." And that's the way it went. When we finished getting the fights into good shape, I set them into their proper continuity in the picture. We then proceeded to work on the rest of the picture.

This was a great way to work, and I was finding out that this guy Zimbalist was a man to be reckoned with. I liked Sam and hoped I would work for him again.

Chapter 6

*T*he Hills of Home, which was made in 1948, was both a period picture and a "Lassie" film. Though certainly no work of art, I remember it for two things. One was the producer, Robert Sisk, a really good guy. He was short and rotund, but not fat. I think I would describe him as being stubby. He was a graduate of Cornell University and erudite to the nth degree. He had a habit of whistling or humming "Far above Cayuga's Waters" all the time.

We got along famously. The first time I had lunch with him, I learned how to eat an entire roll without wasting a crumb. After devouring the roll, he would lick his forefinger and press it to the remaining crumbs on the table. The crumbs would stick to his finger and then the finger would deliver the crumbs to his mouth. I was fascinated. There must be a special course at Cornell to learn how to do this.

Editors always ran dailies with the producer of the previous day's shooting. One day, I sat in the projection room waiting for Sisk to come down from his office and run dailies with me. After an unusually long time, and, anxious to get back to work, I ran up to his office and found him playing gin rummy with screenwriter Dalton Trumbo.

Dalton said, "Look at him, Ralph, I've reduced him to a quivering mass of shit." Well, I fell on the floor, laughing.

Reason number two that made the experience memorable was for a scene shot at night. As we ran the dailies, we saw a medium shot of a group of townsmen standing in a semicircle, talking. Lassie was also in the scene, standing next to her master, Edmund Gwenn. Suddenly, Lassie lifted "her" leg (she was played by a male dog) and peed on Gwenn's pants. Gwenn did not feel a thing because his pants were too thick.

Two takes were printed. Obviously, Fred Wilcox, the director, printed the first take for a gag. The dog did not pee in the second take, because he had voided in the first take and was now quite comfortable. He probably couldn't remember his peeing cue anyway.

Maybe this reason for remembering *The Hills of Home* should be "number one."

1949. The year of *On the Town*. This picture I can only describe as being delicious. I was in complete awe of this group of movie makers: Arthur Freed, Roger Edens, Gene Kelly, Stanley Donen, Conrad Salinger, Saul Chaplin. All wonderful musicians. They never spoke of cuts or scenes, they only spoke of bars and measures. Not being a musician, I was hanging on by my teeth. It had me crazy for a while, but I hung on. Gee, they were great.

On the Town was ticklish to work on. The use of montages is a process of a lot of quick scenes dissolving and cutting one into another telling part of the story quickly in big CU's and inserts, and titles going across the bottom of the screen, including the use of loud sound effects and music. Montages can be very effective and were used quite a lot in the 1930s and 1940s.

Stanley Donen and Gene Kelly directed this movie as their first directorial effort; I thought their work was impeccable. A lot of great musical numbers, and difficult to shoot, too. Stanley Donen went on to a terrific directorial career. Gene Kelly would have been wasted had he continued to direct. He was a such a great dancer.

Roger Edens cornered me on the night of the sneak preview and said, "Ralph, if it wasn't for you, I don't think we could have gotten this picture ready." A slight exaggeration, but it was nice to hear.

Chapter 7

When I first learned that MGM was going to make *King Solomon's Mines*, I went to my boss, Bill LeVanway, and asked to be assigned to the picture. He said, "You'll be through with your present assignment before that picture starts, and I will not have anything to charge your time to while you're waiting." I was so anxious to cut this movie, I offered to take a layoff. Well, I did not get laid off and I did get the assignment.

It was 1949 and *King Solomon's Mines* was my twenty-second credit. Sam Zimbalist was the producer. This picture promised to be a lot of work. An adventure story and Zimbalist. It smelled of excitement and I knew there would not be a dull moment. I was happy.

Sam and I became great friends; he came to my house and I went to his house. When we were away from work, there was lots of joking around and kibitzing—very loose. But once in the screening room or the office to discuss work, everything became very formal. Sam examined every frame, so to speak, and when people came into the screening room to look at his dailies, he brooked no talking from anyone while the film was running.

There is a moment in the picture when Stewart Granger shows Deborah Kerr life in the forest by turning over a fallen tree. Thousands and thousands of bugs are crawling underneath a rotting limb. Granger says, "*Yu yut sava.*" In Swahili, that means, "You eat me. I eat you. We eat them. They eat us. Survival of the fittest." In a way, that became our work ethic.

Sam did not wait for the whole picture to be cut together before he looked at any of it. As soon as a sequence was finished shooting, and I had it cut together, we would immediately sit down and rework it. By the time the picture was finished shooting, we had most of it in very good shape, cutting-wise. After *King Sol* was finally together, we would sit in the screening room and go at the film hammer and tongs, discussing adds and trims, looking, looking, always examining the film for ways to improve.

This picture was put together with spit and bailing wire. By this, I mean with lots of little pieces. It had very few sustained scenes. Sam would say put a shot of this or that into this scene. If I said, "But I don't have such a shot," Sam persisted. "Well, you must have something that will work," he'd say. "Find it." Sam never gave up and he taught me, just by watching him, to be the same way.

When Sam asked for a change in cutting, and I knew it would not work, I'd say, "Gee, Sam, how in the hell am I going to make that work?"

"You will just have to examine it. Get the film in your hands and examine it." Examine, examine, examine. That was his favorite word. And, you know, nine times out of ten, I found something that would work.

You have to approach the job with this attitude: Never let the film whip you. You whip *it*! Never let the film get the best of you. Film is very pliable and some wonderful things can be done with it. Make it do what you want it to do.

There were times, however, when nothing I tried had worked, and that spot in the picture would come up on the screen again, Sam would say nothing and I would say nothing. He knew we had exhausted every possibility.

Sam was fantastic on the editing of action sequences. For example, the stampede sequence for *King Solomon's Mines* was never written into the script. While the company was in Africa, one of the boys started fooling around with his 16mm camera and photographed some shots of animals running here and there. When we saw this stuff on the screen, Sam had the idea of shooting a stampede. He sold the idea to the executives, who dispatched another crew to Africa to shoot the stampede.

Later, after the company returned home, it was discovered that some close shots of the cast were needed for the editing. A flock of sheep was painted with black stripes to look like zebras. Then they were forced to jump over the cast, who lay behind their equipment, using it as a barricade against the onrushing animals. These new pieces became very quick, close, flash cuts on the screen, maybe eight or ten frames in length, and we got away with it—the audience never knew these animals were sheep.

Zimbalist liked music, but he was always concerned that music distracted too much from the dialogue. I think he was right. Even today some pictures play the music too loud under dialogue scenes, making the words unintelligible.

Sam's philosophy was, You can release a picture without music, but you cannot release it without dialogue.

Johnny Green was the head of the MGM music department at the time *King Sol* was coming to its final cut. Johnny met with Sam and said, "It's about time we discussed the music for the picture." Sam said, "What music? We're going to use all the marvelous chants that were recorded by the natives in Africa." I was privy to this meeting and I thought Johnny was going to split a gut. But he could not talk Sam out of the chants. And that's the way the picture was released. As it turned out, the chants were terrific and they lent a lot of quality and African flavor to the picture.

This movie was a joy to work on, especially with Zimbalist, who was a great help to me. The result of all of this effort was most gratifying, because the picture turned out great and was a big hit at the box office. The picture was nominated by the Academy that year for best picture, photography, and editing. It won for editing and photography.

Sam Zimbalist asked me to go to Rome and edit *Quo Vadis,* which was to be his next picture. I accepted the assignment with alacrity. My third daughter was on the way. Gee whiz! I was gonna pay for three weddings someday. Sam asked me if I had ever flown in a commercial airplane. I never had. "Hell, Ralph, it's just like sitting in this office." It turned out to be the bumpiest ride I ever had on an airplane. My old Chevy was a pretty bumpy ride, too.

Chapter 8

1950. *Quo Vadis.* On my way to Italy, I stopped in London to look at some editorial equipment, then flew to Rome in a Lancaster bomber that the Brits had converted into a small commercial plane. Some of the seats in the middle of the cabin were set in a square that was conducive to pleasant conversation with the other passengers. It was five pm and we were flying at about 7,000 feet as we made our approach into Rome. The sun was low, throwing its rays across the city and bathing everything in a lovely peach color. The Coliseum looked like a cup and saucer in the setting sun.

Rome is a very beautiful city and I never could get enough of it. The studio, Cinecittá, a vast place with big flowing lawns, was built on the outskirts of Rome in Mussolini's time. Extremely spacious, it had been used as a camp for displaced persons after the war and there were still quite a lot of these people hanging around all the time. None of them spoke English, but at night there were always a few of them standing near our doorway watching us work, making it an interesting place to make a movie.

The stages were built out of stone. The cutting rooms had their own building with ten large rooms, five on each side of a very wide corridor. Heavy battleship linoleum ran throughout and was kept at a high polish by a young man named Mario Gatti. I loved him for the way he toiled and serviced us. He was in his twenties and could not speak one word of English. We couldn't even teach him to say "yes." I tipped him 300 lira a week, big man that I was. Well, hey, it amounted to about fifty cents. The fellows in my crew also tipped him. We used to have so much fun kidding around with this sweet human being. My assistant editor, Hugo Grimaldi, an Italian, did the translating.

Mario lived in a stone house with his wife and baby. When the baby

35

got sick and needed penicillin, which Mario could not afford, we all chipped in and bought it for him. Some time later, he came in with some homemade cordial for us all to drink a toast on his baby's first birthday. We stopped work and sat around for a few minutes toasting this joyous moment.

I came back to Rome three more times, the first after an eight-year lapse. Mario was still there and we renewed our friendship. Then, again after another four years, and this sweet guy was still there. What nostalgia. When we came back the last time, ten years had slipped by. Although I was in another studio, I inquired and tried and tried, but could not find him. He still holds a special place in my heart.

Mervyn LeRoy, the director on *Quo Vadis,* also wanted me on the picture. I had already edited two pictures for him—*Little Women* and *Any Number Can Play*—and I knew him well. He was a rather small, cocky man, with a nice complexion. He stuttered a bit, especially when he got excited, and he always had a long thin cigar in his mouth. A sensitive, petulant little bastard, he had a wonderful way of keeping all his underlings in a constant state of tension. He also had many spies around the studio lot who told him what was going on. Even in Rome he wanted to know everyone's business.

In those days, relationships were more formal, and I usually addressed my bosses as "Mr." That relationship changed while we were waiting for the first day's dailies to come back from London. The exposed negative, which was shipped to the lab in London for development and printing, was supposed to get back to Rome within four days. Everyone was on pins and needles to see the first dailies.

As the fourth day wore on, we learned we would not be receiving any film on that day. I went down to the set where LeRoy was directing a scene with Deborah Kerr and Robert Taylor. I relayed this information to LeRoy and also told him I was going into Rome.

"What are you going into Rome for?" he wanted to know.

"I want to get a look at the city," I told him. "And . . . I need a haircut."

Well, you would have thought I hit him. "I'm trying to shoot a delicate scene," he whined, "and he needs a haircut."

Deborah Kerr walked away. Robert Taylor went in another direction. Robert Surtees, the cameraman, disappeared behind the camera. I was so embarrassed, I could feel my face turning a fiery red.

"I don't have to go, Mr. LeRoy," I said, and quietly walked off the set. I wished I was back home where I could quietly go to my own barber, Cicero Dutra, and get a haircut.

About fifteen minutes later, I got a call from the assistant director. "Mr. LeRoy says it's okay for you to go into the city."

"I lost my ride," I said. "And please tell Mr. LeRoy to go to hell." I never forgave him for that and I never cut another picture for him, either. From that day on, I called him "Merv."

Later, when Merv, Sam Zimbalist, and I were working on the picture in a screening room at MGM in Culver City, we came to a spot where the camera was shooting down into a deep pit over the heads of the actors. The actors were standing in the shot as the action started. The wild bull that Ursus was going to fight in the arena was kept in this pit. Merv suggested that we add the actors' entrance to the shot. Merv's mechanics were very good and he always had his actors make entrances into and exits out of scenes, but not this time. The reason was that the actors had to be set carefully into the scene in order not to block the camera from seeing the bull. I guess Merv forgot.

I had already been over this with Sam at a previous run and so I said, "They do not make an entrance. They are already in position as the scene starts."

Merv leapt to his feet, proclaiming, "I always shoot entrances and exits, don't I, kid?" He pulled out a wad of bills that would choke a horse and offered to bet me any amount that the actors make an entrance into the shot.

Boy, did I have him. I was going to put on an act and bet him fifty cents, but before I could open my mouth, Sam says, "Shut up, Mervyn. They don't enter. Sit down." Merv sat down as though he were being lowered by a rope.

Before we left Rome, fourteen of us had an audience with Pope Pius XII. It was arranged for a Sunday during the shooting of the picture. We went to the Vatican, where we were led down a long corridor with many small rooms leading off a lovely, sunlit hall, and into a room that was beautifully furnished and decorated. We were made to stand in a horseshoe formation.

Eddie Mannix, the boss, was first in line, then came Sam Zimbalist, Deborah Kerr, Robert Taylor, Mervyn LeRoy, and the rest of us around the semicircle. The cameraman, Bob Surtees, and I were standing next to each other on the other side of the room. We were all breathless and excited. Then, there was a moment's wait. The Pope swept into the room. He was beautifully gowned and had a jeweled skullcap on. He was very slight and very thin with a dark complexion, and he wore rimless glasses on his aquiline nose, but there was an aura about him. He was followed by two other gowned men.

Mannix dropped to his knees and kissed the Pope's ring. The Pope said a few words to him that I could not distinguish. Next, he stepped over to Sam and asked if he were the leading man in the picture. Bob Surtees whispered to me, "The Pope must think we're making a horror picture." A big sob welled up in my throat and I let out a very low scream. My face swelled up and I could feel it getting flushed. Thank God I was able to control myself to a degree.

The Pope continued around the room saying a few words to everyone. When he got to me, he asked in perfect English, "What do you do for the picture?"

"I am the film editor, your holiness." He gave me a little smile and swept on. As he was leaving the room, he stopped, turned, and raised his hands and blessed us. It was quite an afternoon.

There is a moment in *Quo Vadis* when the Christians are led into the arena and the trumpets blare out a tremendous fanfare. The time allowed for these fanfares was sixteen seconds—that's twenty-four feet of film. Nothing was etched in stone, but Sam felt that was all the time the audience needed to look at fanfares. Miklos Rozsa, who was doing the music for the picture, came to me and said he needed twenty-four seconds for the fanfares to sound decent. He wanted twelve more feet added, which would be eight seconds added into that series of cuts so he could do it.

Not unmindful of Sam's aversion to music, I said, "Micky, I know it will be better, and I will add the footage. But if Sam notices it, I'm a dead man." I added the footage and the fanfares sounded great. Luckily, Sam never noticed—or if he did, he never said a word.

When we were mixing *Quo* in the sound department, Sam and Douglas Shearer, the brother of Norma Shearer and head of the sound department, got into a slight brouhaha about balance between the music and dialogue. Sam always wanted the music to be lower and Doug wanted it to be higher.

Finally, Doug said, "If you don't watch the screen and bend down and put your head between your legs and just listen, you can make a lot better judgment of the balance."

"Audiences watch the screen," Sam argued. "I can't imagine them with their heads between their legs." Of course, Sam won the argument. I sat very still but I was bursting inside.

Zimbalist loved to play all kinds of practical jokes on people. I'm reminded of the time he hired an actor, who spoke English with a slight foreign accent, to pose as a renowned sound man from South America. Sam then invited Doug Shearer, who was an awful square, to have lunch with them. Well, this guy started to ride Doug, saying that the Americans knew nothing about sound and that all they knew how to do was to turn on "click-knobs" and make noise. As the luncheon wore on, this fellow was getting under Doug's skin and they got into a horrible argument while Sam was splitting his sides. He finally had to separate them.

I fell in love with the word "click knob," and it became part of my vocabulary from that moment on.

I mention this incident because Mervyn LeRoy was meat for Sam. In fact, he was a juicy T-bone steak. Sam hated the fact that every time we'd go to the screening room to look at the dailies that came in from London, we would no sooner get started when here would come Mervala (Merv). He would simply leave the set, which was a no-no. This infuriated Sam, who felt that he, Sam, was entitled to look at dailies with some degree of privacy.

So one day when we started to run the dailies, Sam locked the door. Pretty soon, up came Mervala. He tried to open the door, except that it wouldn't open. He banged and yelled for about two minutes while Sam motioned for me to be quiet. Pretty soon, Mervy went away. He never tried that again.

Mervyn printed a lot of takes on certain scenes. When Sam and I looked at the dailies, he would make *his* choices, saying if Merv's choices differed, let him know. Of course, Merv would always look at his dailies at the end of shooting every day but he hated to pick takes the first time he looked. He always said, "I'll pick them later, kid."

Every day I would get after him to look at the film and pick his takes, as I kept falling behind in my work, but Mervyn just couldn't make the decision. One day, Sam asked me how the cutting was going. When I told him I was waiting for the great man to pick takes, he blew his stack. "Start cutting," Sam ordered. "Use my picks."

I gleefully set to work. Now I stopped begging Mervyn to pick takes. After a day or two, he asked me how things were going. I blithely said, "Just fine." He looked at me kind of funny. I guess he got wise and must have said something to Sam. The next day when he looked at his film, Mervyn said in a really crying voice, "It's a shame that a director can't pick his own takes." I smugly agreed. From then on, he picked them at first look.

Another opportunity to torture Mervyn came when Sam and Mervyn entertained the Roman press at a luncheon in the studio. Everyone sat at a long table with the two hosts at each end. Pretty soon a messenger came in and handed Sam a telegram. He took it, signed for it, and, without opening it, stuck it in his pocket.

Mervyn went crazy. From the other end of the table he screamed, "Aren't you going to read it?"

"It's none of your business," Sam shot back. Of course, the telegram was a fake. Mervy put his food in his ear during the rest of the luncheon.

Sam also used to tell me stories about card games with Mervyn and the production executive, Henry Henigson. They liked to meet up in their suites on weekends and play gin rummy. On occasion, Sam would have the fake telegram brought in. He wouldn't even look at it, just stuff it in his pocket or throw it on the floor. El Mervo would always say, "Sam, aren't you going to read it?"

"Nah."

From then on, Merv couldn't see his own cards.

Chapter 9

We returned home from Rome in December 1950, right in the middle of all the hype on the upcoming Oscar race. My previous picture, *King Solomon's Mines,* had been nominated for best picture, best photography, and best editing. I was surprised and thrilled to be nominated for an Academy Award. Twenty-two years had passed since I had thrown the first day's rushes from *Four Walls* into the ash can.

When you are a nominee, the excitement on Oscar night is indescribable. All nominees are seated on the aisles so they can make it quickly to the stage if they are called. For most of the evening, I was in a fog. When the editing award was about to be announced, I froze. I heard my name read, but I couldn't move a muscle. My wife, Teddy, poked me. "Get up," she whispered, "You won."

I was comatose as I got out of my seat and started down the aisle toward the stage. All I thought was, "Don't fall down going up the steps to the stage."

The Oscar was thrust into my hands. I croaked out a "Thank you" and was led from the stage. My picture was taken. It was a terrifying experience. As soon as I regained my composure, I looked for my parents. I knew exactly where my mother and dad were supposed to be sitting and I stopped at their seats for a big hug and kiss. Their Ralphie was forty-one and a half. The thrill, the excitement, the joy of winning an Academy Award. Number one. Head of the class. Cock-of-the-walk.

One year later and I was nominated again, this time for *Quo Vadis.* Gee, two years in a row. Pretty exciting. Hey, I thought, this is easy. I'm a cinch. After all, I had just won an Oscar the previous year.

Quo Vadis was up against *A Place in the Sun,* which won. Was I ever shocked. Winning is ecstasy. Losing is agony, especially when you think you have a real chance of winning. *Sun* was a beautiful movie but, in my opinion, not an editorial achievement. Of course, there were three other pictures nominated. I thought *An American in Paris* was a beautiful cutting job. *The Well,* a real dog, got in. Gimme a break! *The African Queen,* which was a real tough job, well cut, and a heck of a good film, never even got nominated.

There is a stench about losing in this kind of competition that lasts. I was down in the dumps for days. I went into a corner and licked my wounds. So it goes. But this was not to be my last chance for glory—or defeat.

In 1953, *Kiss Me Kate* was shot in three-dimensional cinematography. This movie was a lot of fun to work on, but very tricky because of the technology.

Creating the effect required two cameras set next to each other with the lenses about two feet apart; two negatives rolling at the same time and interlocked; and two sets of dailies coming into the cutting room, one set from each camera. It would be hard to tell the difference between the two sets with the naked eye.

Double film also meant double work, editorially speaking. I had to cut one version as though it were not shot in 3-D. Then the assistants had to match the 3-D version to the way my version was cut, and to be very careful not to get the two versions mixed up during the cutting process. That would be chaos.

Now we had two pictures, that were identical, cut for cut. These pictures had to be projected together from two separate projection machines, interlocked, set up two feet apart and viewed with one red lens and one blue lens to get the feeling of depth.

It was really a lot of fun and a real challenge. But after all that work, the studio released the picture straight—as a regular movie with no 3-D effects. Once in a while an art theater runs the picture in 3-D.

That same year we made a trilogy, *The Story of Three Loves,* three good stories and darned good entertainment. The producer, Sidney Franklin, was a fussy little guy, very small in stature, with black hair and a sallow complexion. If you can imagine the look of a prune, that was Mr. Franklin. He had a special jacket that he wore in the projection room. He would put it on so as not to soil himself when he sat where other people had sat.

But I liked Sidney Franklin. He was a gentleman. Soft-spoken and erudite. When he and his writers finished a script, it read like a novel and not a manuscript. He ranked very high in filmdom and had a great record. To name some of his movies: *The Guardsman, The Barretts of Wimpole Street, The Good Earth, Ninotchka, Random Harvest,* and *The Miniver Story.*

I liked to work for him because I respected his brilliance. He and Margaret Booth enjoyed a very close relationship and he would not make a move, editorially speaking, without her input. She chose the editors on his pictures and supervised the editing on them. Nothing was too good for Sidney.

Even though I had won two Academy Awards, I was flattered to think that I had finally risen to the pinnacle of the editorial world in Margaret's estimation. She wanted me to edit all the pictures that she supervised. She was the queen and I was the crown prince. As it happened, I did *Young Bess* and *The Story of Three Loves* for Sidney Franklin. Just two. Both just fair.

The Story of Three Loves told three separate tales, separate and apart from one another, story-wise. The three tales needed to be tied together somehow. There was no point of view (POV), creating a documentary feel to them. After the picture was finished and cut together, it lacked a unifying point of view.

Someone came up with the idea that the three groups from the three stories should be set on a cruise on the same ship. Each story would be told from the POV of each couple. The three casts were called together and retakes were made.

Vincente Minelli, a very talented director, directed one episode. Gottfried Reinhardt directed two episodes. Reinhardt was a wonderful man. Big, dark of complexion, beetle-browed, roly-poly, and erudite. We became very good friends. I loved being around him.

The story now started on the ship with a short scene between James Mason and Moira Shearer and then their story was told. After that, we came back to the ship to meet couple number two, Leslie Caron and Farley Granger, and we got their story. Finally, we went back to the ship again for the last story, played by Kirk Douglas and Pier Angeli. In a way, it seemed to work pretty good. One got the feeling that the three stories *were* tied together somehow. Why is it that any story, in movies or books or any medium, is stronger when told from someone's point of view? I don't know. But it is. Every time I could cut a scene and make it play from someone's POV, the scene played infinitely better.

One of the great examples of cause and effect, points of view, and reaction shots, was the movie *Shane.* In this picture, watching Shane, and seeing him and all the fighting from the little boy's point of view was an absolutely marvelous way of telling the story. I wish I had edited *Shane,* a truly great job of movie making.

Executive Suite was another very enjoyable assignment. Robert Wise was the director. A real heavyweight. At one time in his career, he was a film editor, and the editor of *Citizen Kane.* His directorial credits are sensational: *West Side Story, I'll Cry Tomorrow, The Sound of Music,* and more. Great, entertaining movies.

Directors and producers who at one time in their careers were editors naturally understand editorial problems. Bob Wise knew exactly what he needed in the way of angles in order for a scene to be cut properly. It was a pleasure to cut for this man.

During the shooting, Bob would come into the studio at three o'clock in the morning and lay out his work for the day. By the time the crew and cast arrived, he was ready. Quite a work ethic, I'd say. Of course, he went to bed every night at eight o'clock.

Executive Suite, a talkie in every sense of the word, had a chance to be a very static motion picture. A lot of the picture took place around a long table used for conferences, and the story was overladen with dialogue. Robert Wise, thinking and knowing that movement of the camera would keep the picture from having a static feel, had the camera moving whenever he could. This definitely did heighten the feeling of motion and kept the picture from having a static feel.

I thought this movie was beautifully directed.

Also in 1953, I had the great pleasure of working with Stanley Donen again, this time on *Seven Brides for Seven Brothers.* A slim, rather tall fellow with black hair, Stanley was an extremely talented man. At one time in his career he had been a dance director and choreographer.

We got along just fine, and I thought the preparation on this movie was nothing short of brilliant. Every one of the musical numbers in this picture was planned out very carefully before shooting. Each angle was shot with a very short overlap into the next angle. There was a specific place to make the cut into the next shot. I had a ball cutting the musical numbers because they were planned out so well for shooting and cutting.

The movie had great direction by Donen and the great work of the dance director, Michael Kidd, a stocky, interesting man with an open face and a sweet disposition. The work of these two men made this a very enjoyable picture to work on.

It was not a tough movie to cut. Yet, mainly because of the great way it was shot, the picture was nominated for an Academy Award for best editing. Naturally, I was delighted to be nominated again.

Perhaps if the movie had been released in a year where the competition was not so strong, this simple little musical might have won an Academy Award for editing. But the excellent movie, *On the Waterfront,* swept the Oscars, walking off with eight statuettes that night.

But once having been nominated there is, as I explained earlier, tremendous disappointment when you don't get the award. Instead, you have to be Mr. Nice Guy and go to the ball and smile and keep saying "Better luck next time." My aching back!

Once an editor gets nominated into the first five, having been put there by his peers, it's truly an honor—a great honor. After all, it gives you something nice to think about while you're in a corner, licking your wounds.

My next film, *Jupiter's Darling,* was anything but "darling." It is said that an editor can make or break a film. Don't believe it. This picture was badly broken without any help from anyone—a real dog.

I was stuck on this turkey for eight months, but the people who made the picture really were darling. Howard Keel and Esther Williams starred, while George Sydney, a really swell guy and very nice to work for, directed. He was heavyset but good looking with even features, and he was always smoking a pipe. George made some great musicals for MGM, but he fell on his face with this bomb.

I did get two benefits out of this experience. First, Howard Keel and I became very good friends. The second thing was that I learned something new, as I always do on a picture, though it took me a quarter of a century to realize it on this one.

There's a scene in the movie where the background was a forest. Esther and Howard were sitting on a big stump of a big tree, and there was lots of dialogue going on. The first angle shot was a full figure angle of the action. The second angle was exactly the same but much closer to the actors. Both angles were shot straight on. Now, it's always smoother when changing angles—that is, making a cut to another angle—if the new angle is three-quarters on, rather than shot straight on, as this scene was.

I started the scene in the full shot, and at a certain point in the dialogue, I cut to the closer angle just to get close to the actors. Not too great dramatically, but smooth anyway. Margaret Booth was supervising. She suggested another place in the scene to cut in. I examined the place she chose and did not like it much either. I did not make the change. The next time we ran the picture, she stopped the film at this same place. As though she had never said a word, she suggested cutting in at her previously suggested place.

When I got back to the cutting room and examined the spot, I thought it would make an awful cut. Not wanting to get my head lopped off, I decided to do it. I closed my eyes and made the cut.

The next time we ran the picture, Margaret stopped at the same place, and as if nothing had ever been said about that particular cut, she said, "I think that's a very good cut." Personally, I thought it was ugly. I thought the

cut jumped all over the screen. The producer and the director were not disturbed. At the preview, as the cut went by, the audience didn't stir.

Twenty-five years later, I see that *Jupiter's Darling* is going to be on television. Twenty-five years! I've got to see that cut again. I am sitting in front
of my TV. The picture comes on. I wait with bated breath. Here comes the
cut! It goes by as smooth as glass. Hmmmm.

Chapter 10

In 1956, I worked on a very enjoyable movie called *High Society,* a remake of *The Philadelphia Story.* I considered this to be a plum assignment and looked forward to working on it.

I slipped back in my mind's eye sixteen years to when *The Philadelphia Story* was made. 1940. I was a thirty-one-year-old stripling, just starting to edit. Frank Sullivan, a truly great editor whose work I admired greatly, was the editor on *The Philadelphia Story.* Every producer and director on the lot were always happy when Frank Sullivan was assigned to edit their picture.

I hung around Frank, hoping some of his talent would rub off on me. He was not a big man physically. His hair was always unruly, never combed. He had a dark complexion and many great big blackheads were liberally sprinkled across his face. Actually, you could have shot them off with a BB gun. There was so much hair coming out of his nose, you could have shot a Tarzan picture in there. On a hot day, the sweat stains on his shirt came down in a great semicircles from his armpits. I never saw him with a jacket on.

One day when I walked into his cutting room, he was doodling on the light box on his bench. Great stacks of film rolls were on his bench waiting to be edited. I asked, "Why are you doing that with so much work to be done?"

"I am trying to figure out how to cut this sequence," he said, "and doodling helps me to think." I thought, I'd doodle all day long if I could cut that well. Anyway, back to my narrative.

In a way, I felt as though I were stepping into Frank's shoes by editing the remake of *The Philadelphia Story.* I felt honored, thrilled, and excited.

High Society was not officially a musical, but it had some terrific music in it. The director, Charles Walters, was a good-looking, slightly built man and a hell of a nice guy. Originally a dancer and choreographer, he came from the New York stage.

Unfortunately, most of the directors who come to movies with only stage experience are so steeped in directing for the stage they do not know how to use the film medium. The varieties of camera angles that can come into play are a tremendous boon to storytelling on the screen. But when Charles shot a scene for a movie, it was like looking at the action from the first row in a theater. From an editor's point of view, Charles' mechanics were therefore very simple.

One night after we ran dailies, I showed him a sequence, newly edited, where Frank Sinatra sings the love song "You're Sensational" to Grace Kelly. Charles liked the cutting but suggested going into a close-up of Frank at a point in the scene where a sexy saxophone phrase of the music came in.

It would have been much too early to cut to the close-up, I explained, as it would make the cutting look choppy, but Charles kept saying he wanted the close-up on this phrase of the music. I kept demurring and finally he got up and said "Fuck it!" And he left the projection room.

I was shocked. I jumped up and ran after him saying that I would certainly try and fix the cut to his satisfaction. But he kept walking and saying, "Fuck it." After shooting all day, a director, who is tired and has been handling temperamental actors, doesn't need his editor to argue with him. I might add: his editor who should know better. I was devastated and just could not come to grips with this happening. I was so upset, I broke down in the middle of dinner that evening right in front of my wife and three kids. I never slept a wink.

The next morning when I entered the studio, as luck would have it, I ran smack into Sol Siegel, the producer of the picture. I explained what had happened and assumed all the blame. I asked him to take me off the picture, as I was sure that Walters would not want me on it after what had happened the night before. Sol calmed me down and said he would talk to Walters.

A little later, Sol called me and said that Walters would have no part of my leaving the picture. In fact, Charles had insisted that I remain as the editor. I was very surprised, not to mention relieved and happy. I said that I would never argue with a director again. I went down to the set later in the day to see him. We both sort of looked at each other and neither of us said a word. I was too embarrassed and he was too busy. He was a good guy.

You just can't cut into music like dialogue. It occurred to me that if the music were longer, I could make the cut a bit later, the way Walters wanted it. I went to see my music editor on the picture, a brilliant man with music, Bill Saracino, who physically spread the music by adding four bars.

That way, I was able to get into Frank's close-up four bars later. Right where Charles wanted it. Hallelujah!

Sol Siegel showed me another side of his personality one night after a tough session in the projection room. When we went up to his office to discuss changes, Sol pulled a bottle of Scotch out of his desk and poured himself a healthy slug. Can you believe he never even asked me to have a glass of water? Mr. Yifnif.

Yifnif is a Yiddish slang word meaning, "stuck up," "wise guy," "know it all." A superior person, sarcastically speaking, of course. Every Jewish family has their own array of expressions. It can get pretty complicated sometimes.

Chapter 11

*B*en-Hur—the assignment of the century! What a picture! What a moment
in my life. What an experience. I was thrilled and excited to get this plum.
And very happy that Sam Zimbalist wanted me. I had worked very hard on
the other pictures I had edited for Sam and felt that I deserved the assignment.
And I really think all my fellow editors at MGM were glad for me.

As soon as I was assigned to edit *Ben-Hur*, I told Sam I wanted to take
an American assistant editor along. This meant the studio would have to
spring for a higher salary than the Italian assistant editors got, plus the cost of
transportation, per diem, etc. It was quite an item and Sam didn't think the
executives would go for it.

"Sam, I can't go to Rome and do all the editing without an American
assistant," I explained. "And when we get home with all the film, I will be
the only one in the cutting room who knows the film. It won't work."

"You mean to tell me you won't go unless you can take an assistant?"
Sam asked.

I was startled by the question. With a lot of false bravado, I said, "That's
right." I wanted to do the picture in the worst way and Sam knew it. He also
knew I would waver, but he also knew I was right. He just wanted to be able
to go upstairs and say, "Ralph won't go without an assistant and I want
Ralph." Period. And by taking that position with the executives, Sam got
the mission accomplished.

Nineteen-fifty-eight was a very emotional year for me. Very high and
very low. My father was quite ill, and when the time came for my departure
to Rome, I hesitated to leave. The doctors told me not to worry, to go ahead,
that Dad would still be here when I came home.

Five days after I got to Rome, the fateful telegram arrived. My dad had died. If I had only known, I could have waited the few days. It was a very upsetting start for this gigantic assignment. I was glad and thankful that I had my wife and three daughters with me. They were wonderful.

After the first unit had been filming for about two weeks, the chariot race unit started shooting the chariot race. For the first three months of shooting, I worked on nothing else but the chariot race. This sequence had a separate script, a separate shooting unit, its own director, a stunt director, and its own crew.

An interesting sidelight: Only one half of a circus maximus was built for the chariot race. Although the set was actually larger than the real Coliseum, still, only one half of the arena was built. Therefore the company had only one side of the arena to shoot in. There were five thousand extras sitting in the grandstand, but only on one side. In order to get the feeling of the chariots circling the arena, the cameras would shoot from one end of the arena with the chariots racing up that side. Most of the shots were angled on to the oncoming chariots with some shots angled toward the spina and CUs to be intercut with the action.

As they came to the end of the spina, a high angle would be used, shooting down. Now the theater audience sees them make their turn. Now they are racing down the other side of the spina—or so it seems. They are really racing back down the first side. The shot that showed them make the turn completed the illusion of circling.

The side of the arena the company was shooting only had the sun in the morning, so any afternoon shooting would be in the shade. In cutting the sequence, many times sunny shots would be intercut with shady shots. It couldn't be helped; but, interestingly enough, it never bothered the audience.

The principal actors, Charlton Heston as Ben-Hur, and Stephen Boyd as Messala, were being used every day with the first unit, and doubles were used for long shots and medium shots for the chariot race. This inhibited the start of editing, as there were no close-ups of the principals to intercut in the assembling of the sequence. However, the shooting schedule called for the race unit to get Heston and Boyd for close-ups a little later.

When the chariot race unit did get access to the two principals, they discovered that both actors could drive the chariots. It is very difficult to handle a team of four horses and requires a lot of strength. It was quite a boon for the camera, and many of the medium-sized angles already taken with the doubles were retaken, using Heston and Boyd themselves. The boys gave me a ride on a chariot one day. I thought my back would break. I decided to stay in the cutting room and ride the Moviola.

Someone once asked me how in the world did I start to cut this sequence. I explained that as soon as the first day's dailies came in, which could only be a few shots at a time, you put them together. And day by day, as the footage accumulates, you put the pieces together. Working the new shots in and reworking all the shots. And day by day the sequence grows. I fibbed a little bit. Actually, I had to wait until the first four or five day's shooting accumulated in order to get a good start on the cutting.

In addition, I had a big chart of each lap of the race pinned up on the wall. I was able to keep a record of what went into each lap. It was a big help as the race was not shot in continuity.

I started to put this sequence together with some trepidation. It took seven days and nights just to throw parts of it together into the roughest kind of shape so we could get a look at it and start to get the feel of the sequence to see how it was going. There were nine teams of horses: thirty-six principals and thirty-six doubles. In addition, there were three teams of Ben-Hur's whites and three teams of Messala's blacks. Counting all the ponies and horses that the cowboys rode, there were nearly one hundred horses altogether. A veritable race track stable on the back lot of Cinecitteá. It was pretty funny to see these cowboys with their Stetsons and boots and bow legs walking the streets of the Eternal City.

On one of the turns during the race, the chariots driven by Heston and Boyd bumped together, nearly causing an unstaged accident. When we saw the dailies on this scene, Zimbalist had close-ups made of Heston and Boyd to intercut and dramatize this moment.

People have often said that someone was killed during the shooting of the race. That is not true. The worst accident was suffered by Heston's double, who cut his chin when he was thrown over the front of Ben-Hur's chariot. This was truly an accident—not staged and no one was killed. However, Sam did ask that a close-up be made of Heston climbing back into the chariot to intercut with the "accident."

When the sequence was finally finished shooting, we wound up with about 60,000 feet of film and about 450 separate shots. To save money, these scenes were printed in black and white, since color prints were more expensive. That meant I had to memorize the look of each driver without the benefit of seeing their colorful costumes. I worried that when we put the color in after it was cut together, it would have a different look, and because of the color, some shots would need lengthening, or maybe trimming.

Normally, in a sequence where there are a lot of colorful costumes and a lot of movement, some shots may need to be on the screen a little less or a little more than a black and white print so that the audience gets just the right amount of time to look at the shot. There is just no pattern to this possible problem.

If the chariot race had been printed in color instead of black and white in the first place, the hair-pulling would not have been necessary.

When something of interest happens on the screen, like two chariots colliding, or Ben-Hur being whipped by Messala, or some kind of spill, we cut to someone in the stands reacting to what they just saw. This cut is called a reaction shot. Reaction shots in any kind of action sequence help to dramatize the moment. It gives the viewer a point of view, which, as I said earlier, is very important for the enjoyment of the audience, because it shows the cause (action) and effect (reaction). In this sequence, the cuts to the sheik in the stands worked very well. Reaction shots should be on the screen just long enough to register with the audience.

The race was an extremely difficult sequence to cut, but the result was most gratifying. In fact, it was truly sensational. Some of the cuts were no more than eight frames in length. Eight frames is one-third of a second on the screen, yet these shots registered with the audience, which shows that a rhythm can be created in the cutting. One way to do this is to slowly reduce the length of each cut in a given series of cuts, which helps to get the eyes of the audience used to the rapid change in the cutting. This is one of the great secrets of fine editing. Zimbalist was an unbelievable help in this process. Without his expertise, this sequence would never have turned out as well as it did. William Wyler, the director, never saw the race until it was complete, but when he did see it, he was very impressed.

An interesting opportunity to embellish the opening parade of chariots presented itself. As the charioteers enter the arena, they go around one bend in the arena and come to a stop in the middle of the track, in front of the royal box. In my mind's eye, I pictured it as the equivalent of a six-furlong race at a race track. We all thought the parade to the royal box was so beautiful it should continue until the chariots made one complete circle of the arena. This we could accomplish because there was so much film available on the sequence. I pictured it as a mile-and-a-quarter race at a race track. It worked beautifully in the film. Of course, there were no hoofprints in the sand in the unused portion of the track. Remember, they only went around one turn. But we got away with it. Some man, somewhere, did pick up on it and he was the only person, as far as I know, who caught on. He wrote Willy Wyler a letter about it and Willy turned the letter over to me. I did nothing about it. What could I do?

The first sequence shot in the entire picture was a scene at supper. Ben-Hur, his sister, and mother are eating. All the angles were shot straight on and in the aspect ratio of three to one. To put it simply, the image was three times as long as it was tall—a very wide rectangle—three across and one down, but not conducive to good composition. Wyler was going crazy trying to make it look like something. The actress who was then playing the part of the mother was pretty bad, too. When the film came back from the lab (Technicolor now had a laboratory in Rome), Wyler asked me to cut the sequence together so we could see what it looked like. Well, it did not look good. I didn't think the cutting was good, but neither was the scene. I showed the sequence to Wyler. He left the projection room without a word.

The next day, Zimbalist said to me, "Willy did not like the way you cut that scene." I could not believe my ears. I became terribly upset. I offered to get off the picture, but Sam tore me apart. "Wanna pick up your marbles and go home?" he asked me sarcastically. Boy, did he give me hell. I felt like a fool.

Sam thought I ought to talk to Wyler about the "complaint." Wyler had had his own editor for his many pictures in the past. His name was Robert Swink, a fine editor, a swell fellow, and a good friend of mine, too. I often wondered why he wasn't picked for *Ben-Hur,* but I did not ask any questions. I guess Sam told Wyler in the beginning that he wanted me. It just couldn't be that Willy didn't like my cutting—or could it? Maybe he just wanted his own editor. Sure, that was it. Hmmmm.

That night, I waited for Wyler at the front gate. Pretty soon here comes the big limo taking big Willy home. I flagged him down. He stuck his head out of the window. I said, "Mr. Wyler, Sam told me that you complained to him about the cutting of that scene."

He gulped and said, "Sam was not supposed to say anything to you about that."

"Just the same, Mr. Wyler, when you don't like the way I put a scene together, please tell me and I will recut it any way you like."

He had lost a measure of my respect, and from then on "Mr. Wyler" became "Willy." The result of all this was they reshot the scene and recast the part of the mother. So the problem could not have been just the cutting. Nevertheless, I grieved about this episode for a long time. Later, I realized that Zimbalist probably thought the sequence was bad right from the day he first saw the dailies. As usual, he had played it smart.

One day, I was in the cutting room working away when I got a call from the set. "Mr. Wyler wants to see you right away." I was really up to my hips in work and jealous of every moment away from the cutting room. However, I dashed down to the set.

Willy said, "Ralph, how would you shoot this scene?" The scene is set in a long corridor where Ben-Hur and Messala throw spears into an arch above a doorway.

I swelled up like a balloon. The great Wyler was asking me how to shoot the scene. I immediately went into my best Hollywood stance, holding up my hands shaped the way the scene should be shot; open palms, thumb to thumb. I told him to shoot it this way and that way, suggesting about four angles.

I got all through, and without the slightest hesitation, Wyler said, "That stinks."

I slunk back to my cutting room with my tail between my legs, cursing him all the way. When I saw the film, I realized some of my suggestions *had* been followed, but it was a very confined set anyway, and there wasn't much choice in angles anyhow.

Well, *Ben-Hur* finally finished shooting in January 1959, taking just about eight months to finish the shoot. Nearly 700,000 feet of film were shipped to MGM in Culver City. We all trouped home except Willy, who went to Cloisters for a little rest and some skiing. There were about 30,000 feet of uncut dailies still to be put together, which took about a month to cut together.

Ben-Hur was finally in one piece. We had a movie! Hallelujah!

King Willy came home and we all sat down in a projection room to look at our handiwork. Five and a half hours long, or 29,700 feet in a first cut. Wow! Willy stopped the projector after the first hour. "I can't digest any more of it. One hour is enough. Let's go up to the office and discuss the first hour of our movie." We sat in Willy's office for the next two days talking about the first hour of *Ben-Hur*. He remembered every shot that was used and every cut in the first hour. The son-of-a-gun had a memory like an elephant. I was amazed.

As we finished our first session in his office, Willy said to us in no uncertain terms, "Now go to work on this first hour, but remember, I don't want any of you working on my film when you are tired. Be sure you get plenty of rest. That way you will make less mistakes." This was on a Friday afternoon. We all fled home to a much deserved weekend.

On Monday morning, we were all called on the carpet by J. J. Cohn, the executive in charge of the picture, and caught hell because no work had been done over the weekend. My, my. What bad boys.

Besides being a brilliant director, Wyler had one quality that I admired very much. He wanted everyone working on the picture to be involved. He listened to every suggestion anyone had to make. Nor was he sensitive. You could argue with him about the film to a fare-thee-well and he would listen to everything you had to say. He didn't always accept the suggestions, but he always got a lot of input.

This reminds me of an incident that to this day tickles me. There were always six or seven of us in the room when we were running the picture. We were looking at the sequence where Christ is put up on the cross. Willy said, "Isn't there some way we can shorten this scene? It seems to take forever."

I had an assistant who was a devout Catholic. His name was Bill McMillin, and he had been in Rome with us. He was small physically, low man on the totem pole, and sitting on the end seat in the projection room, but he piped right up. "Willy, you can't do that."

Willy jumped off his throne, walked down to the end seat, bent down over Bill, and snarled, "Why can't we do that?"

Bill calmly replied, "Because everyone knows that Christ said seven things while he was on the cross and you would be the laughingstock of the whole world if you cut into the moment."

Wyler never said a word. He walked back to his seat, sat down, pressed the buzzer, and the picture continued.

On another occasion, we were running the film with Willy's brother, Robert Wyler, a writer who had done some of the dialogue work. During Messala's death scene, he is gasping to Ben-Hur, "You think your mother and sister are dead. . ."

Suddenly, Willy stopped the film and said, "My God, how does Messala know that Ben-Hur thinks his mother and sister are dead?"

We, the audience, knew that Esther had lied about this to Judah. She had told Ben-Hur that his mother and sister were dead. But how would Messala know that? Well, Willy baby proceeded to lay his brother out. Poor guy. How this mistake was Robert Wyler's fault, I'll never know. Anyway, it was decided to make a retake to fix the problem. Willy said, "We will not do anything except have the retake on hand, and if the preview audience picks up on it, we will use it. If they don't, we'll leave it alone."

Of course, no one ever picked up on it.

Of course, the line could have been taken out of the picture in the first place, which would have cured the problem. But no; Willy wanted to fix it. It meant building part of a set. Getting a crew together. And not least of all, getting poor Steve Boyd (Messala) away from whatever he was doing, and costing a bit of money. Rank has its privileges!

Sometimes, events occurring outside of the set affected our production schedule. One day, when Sam and I were looking at the dailies, the film stopped, the lights went up, and all the projectionists come trooping into the screening room. Not one of them spoke English, but somehow they managed to explain that they would be on strike for one hour. It was exactly twelve o'clock. If we come back in one hour, they told us, they would run the film for us. We had to sit around and wait, and I thought Sam would go mad. But sure enough, one hour later they returned and we saw the rest of the film.

Sam's apathy toward music was the complete opposite of Wyler's position. There's a sequence where Tirzah, Ben Hur's sister, accidentally drops the tiles off the roof onto the marching soldiers; after Ben-Hur and the family are arrested, Messala inspects the tiling. Wyler had me lengthen that part of the sequence so that Miklos Rozsa, who was doing the score, could write even more music. Wyler thought this would embellish the moment and create more emotion. I think he was right.

One day, Sam and I were walking on the lot, Sam walking fast, clanging along on his iron heels on the cement path, me talking and practically running to keep up with him. Suddenly, Sam slipped. I reached out and grabbed him. A purely reflex action. I'm sure I kept him from falling, but he just looked at me and never said a word. We walked on, but the moment stayed with me.

Sam and I worked very hard on the chariot race. It was like a ritual. We sat down every morning and ran the race. In the cutting room next to mine, we had a small projection machine. A sort of "home movies" set-up with a three-by-three screen. We could go back and forth; rock and roll, which is the vernacular of the cutting room. We talked cuts. We made notes. We ran. We reran. Late in the morning, we would stop. I would walk Sam to the door of the cutting room and watch him as he strode away, the sound of his iron taps fading away. Work like crazy the rest of the day, making changes in the cutting and adding any new scenes that came from the lab, to get ready for the next day. This went on for three solid months. I never touched another piece of film in the picture during that time.

Finally, Sam announced, "I think we now have it as good as it can get. Order the color prints."

As was my wont, I walked Sam to the door, and I watched him stride away, heels clanging. I noticed that the cuff on his right pant leg was partially turned back and thought he must have gotten dressed in a hurry. I laughed to myself and went back to work.

An hour later the phone rang. The voice at the other end said, "Sam Zimbalist just died."

Sam Zimbalist died in Rome exactly two months before the picture finished shooting. Having lost my dad that year, I felt lost, stripped, alone. I was terribly sad for a long time. I went to a park in Rome the next Sunday, sat down on a bench, and wrote Sam's widow a long letter. The ballpoint pen kept streaking and blotting. For the next two or three years, I periodically visited Sam's grave in Los Angeles.

Ben-Hur swept the Oscars that year. Willy, who was never too nice, complimented me. He said, "Ralph, you really took care of the film." Whatever that meant. He gave me two bottles of booze.

Eleven years later, I was at a party given by the Mirisches after the opening of their *Fiddler on the Roof*. Willy Wyler was there, and I hadn't seen him in all that time. I walked up to him and said, "Willy, who's the greatest film editor in the world?"

Quick as a flash he said, "Bob Swink." Then recognizing me, he sputtered, demurred, and gave me a big "Hello."

Editing *Ben-Hur* took eighteen months from start to finish. It felt like a lifetime, but it turned out to be the highlight of my career. Most gratifyingly, I was nominated and won an Oscar and received lots of kudos. I reveled in it for a long time. I guess I still do.

Chapter 12

I was very let down after *Ben-Hur*. Tremendous activity and pressure for eighteen months, and then—quiet. MGM didn't pay overtime, but for every Saturday and/or Sunday I had worked, I had earned a day off. I had six weeks vacation with pay coming after *Ben-Hur*.

My wife and three kids didn't take too long to pull me out of the doldrums. We had a pug dog, a sweet little guy named Miko. He was a Chinese dog with a Japanese name. He didn't care. Four women in the house with two males—Miko and I never had a chance. Every time there was an argument among them, Miko and I would cower in a corner. But I really enjoyed my family during those six weeks of vacation. And then, back to work.

Butterfield 8, starring Elizabeth Taylor and Laurence Harvey, was my next assignment. Danny Mann, the director, had done a couple of pictures for Paramount but, like Charles Walters, he was from the New York stage and did not know too much about the camera. Danny had a dark complexion. He wore rimless glasses and was slight of build, wiry, muscled, and with thinning black hair. He was a nut on exercise and smoked salmon, which he called the "friendly fat." A great guy and very talented, he told funny stories and was always upbeat.

The producer, Pandro Berman, was short, dark, nice-looking, and a nice man, though very businesslike. When I came to work on the picture, the company was already shooting in New York, which was where the entire movie was made.

Being from the stage, Danny Mann was not used to shooting the proper angles for editing. As soon as we received the first six days of shooting, I cut it together, if you can call it that. You cannot cut two scenes together unless

61

the sizes are different or there is a definite change in angles. Otherwise there are big jumps.

At this point, the Screen Actors Guild went on strike. Ronald Reagan, then a good Democrat, was president of the Guild. The *Butterfield 8* company came home from New York and I sat around for almost three months, waiting for the strike to finish. Loved it. I helped on other movies and cut screen tests. When the strike finished, the company went back to New York to shoot the rest of the picture. It was decided that I should also go back and stay on the set with Danny to see that the proper angles were shot for cutting purposes. Another editor would be putting the picture together for me at home while I was away.

New York, New York. What a blast! Ten weeks! I even learned how to go to work on the subway. We were working on the seventh floor of a big office building. The whole floor was occupied with our picture and all the sets were built on that floor. It seemed funny to come to work on the subway and go up in an elevator to shoot a movie.

An editor working hand in glove with a director on a set has to be very diplomatic in the way he expresses himself about what shots are needed in order for the picture to go together smoothly and properly. Sometimes the director doesn't want to shoot the angles the editor suggests. Things can get pretty sticky. I think it takes great knack and diplomacy for an editor to handle this kind of job.

Paramount Pictures had a policy of having all their editors stay on the sets with the directors for the same purpose, to see that the pictures were covered properly for editing. This meant that the assistant editor would cut the picture together during the shooting schedule. I thought it was a great idea because the editor, during the shooting, could regularly discuss ideas about the story and find out what the director had in mind, cutting-wise, on certain scenes and sequences. At the same time, the editor learned a lot about direction. The assistant editor would also benefit by having the chance to cut during the shoot.

Some directors did not need this help, some did. But for some reason, MGM never implemented this policy, except in rare instances, as with *Butterfield 8.*

Here's how we worked things out on *Butterfield 8:* Danny would rehearse the scene with the actors, then stage the scene as to how he wanted the actors to move. During rehearsal, I made it my business to stay out of the way; I would stand on the edge of the set and watch. When he finished the rehearsal, Danny would call me over and we would then discuss where the camera should be and what was needed to cover the scene properly. This usually took place with the cameraman.

Thank God, Danny and I got along very well. I loved working with him. Danny didn't know much about the camera and he didn't care who knew it. He had absolutely no ego or temperament at all. We formed a great friendship that lasted for many years.

We did not have to work on Saturdays or Sundays, which gave us time for really great sightseeing around New York. Danny lived at the Stanhope Apartments, which were on 86th Street, and I lived at the Hotel Astor near 42nd Street. We usually met and went for long, long walks on the weekends. I was a trim 160 pounds when I came home. I enjoyed this location very much.

And we must have resolved the issue with the camera angles well enough, because the picture proved a box-office success, and Elizabeth Taylor won an Oscar.

Chapter 13

It was 1961 and Danny Gray, my first boss at MGM, had been dead for six years. I was fifty-two. The brash youngster was long gone. Hey, I was getting up there. I wanted to be a director. Of course, everyone who is not a director wants to be a director. So I went to my new boss, Merle Chamberlain, and asked him to go to bat for me.

The company, in effect, told me that they would rather have a good editor than a mediocre director. I saw their point but, naturally, I did not agree with it. MGM was about to start a big TV program at that time and I wanted to be part of it. I had now been with MGM for thirty-three years. And I had been a loyal and hardworking employee for all those years. I also kept in mind that MGM was a loyal employer for all those years, too. But I was determined to give myself a chance.

I asked for a six months' leave of absence, saying that if I did not become a director in that time, I would come home and cut film and be a good boy. After a lot of haggling, the leave was granted. Two days later, my boss, Merle Chamberlain, called to tell me that if I took the leave, I would lose all my benefits and also a fairly big insurance policy. (Now I really missed Danny Gray.)

By now, I had the directorial bit in my teeth and I quit in disgust. I acquired an agent, got all dressed up, and went out into the world of filmdom to hunt for a directorial job. I was well known and had access to a lot of people in the industry. Everyone offered me a job as an editor, but as a director, no way. I was starting to believe that I was wasting my time and the time of others. On some days, I sat around the house in my pajamas, unshaven, and a pain in the neck to the whole family. But they never told me to stop trying.

This went on for almost a year, believe it or not, with no success. I've often wondered, if I had stayed at MGM, would I have gotten the chance to direct at some time later? I'll never know, of course, but what the hell. In the meantime, I ate, and so did my family.

Although I didn't realize it at the time, I was about to enter a most important time in my career. This was due to meeting the Mirisch Brothers: Harold, Marvin, Walter, and little Larry, Walter's son. Three wonderful men and a marvelous boy. Later, when I started to work for them, twelve-year-old Larry would come into my cutting room occasionally. I would run film through the Moviola for him. Today, he is my agent.

The Mirisches were considered the top independent motion picture company in the entire industry, and working for them was considered a feather in one's cap. Harold was the president, Walter the head of creative affairs, and Marvin the money man. They had tremendous integrity and a great name for fair dealing. No airs, no bullshit, just make movies. Which they did to a fare-thee-well.

Robert Relyea, a friend of mine from our MGM days, was working for the Mirisch Company at the time. He called and asked me if I would go to Munich, Germany, to make some censor-required cuts in a Mirisch picture called *Town without Pity*. I agreed to meet Walter and Marvin Mirisch in a cutting room to go over the changes that needed to be made. In came Walter and Marvin coatless, with rolled-up sleeves, ready to look in the Moviola with me. I was startled. Two of the biggest men in the industry acting like ordinary joes. This was a far cry from what I had been used to at MGM where things were quite formal all the time, and the producers always wore suits and ties.

I liked the Mirisches instantly. Walter, a man of medium height, was the studious type: dark, slim, horn-rimmed glasses, nice looking, black hair and plenty of it. This guy had the tenacity of a bulldog. When he got an idea into his head, right or wrong, there was no way known to man to dislodge it. Marvin was shorter and a little pudgy. A very quiet man, he was an absolute gentleman.

Anyway, I flew to Munich and there met the director of *Town without Pity*, Gottfried Reinhardt, my old friend from *The Story of Three Loves*. He did not want the censor cuts made. I explained that I was told that if the censor cuts were not made, the picture could not be released. Reinhardt finally agreed. He then took me to lunch at a charming café. We started to eat at one o'clock in the afternoon and did not finish until five. Then we went out to dinner. Needless to say, I came home a little heavier than when I left. While coming back on Lufthansa from Munich to New York, I got smashed

With Mama, 1909.

As an extra in Valencia, *1927.*

With Father, 1936.

With Angela Lansbury, Gaslight, 1944.

With Oscar for King Solomon's Mines, *1951.*

At the IATSE dinner for the crew of Quo Vadis, *1950. Sam Zimbalist is in the foreground, Eddie Mannix is on his right, and I am second from the far right.*

With John Dunning and Barbara Rush, Ben-Hur, 1960.

With Dean Martin, Ada, 1961.

Left to right, Harold, Walter, and Marvin Mirisch, circa 1963.

In Paris, The Great Race, *1964.*

With Norman Jewison, Gaily Gaily, 1969.

With Charlton Heston, Walter Mirisch, and Phil Lathrop, The Hawaiians, 1972.

With Billy Wilder and Jack Lemmon, Avanti, 1972

With Jack Lemmon, Avanti, 1972.

With Billy Wilder and I.A.L. Diamond, Front Page, *1974.*

With Blake Edwards at the Olivetti Estate, Curse of the Pink Panther, *1981.*

on champagne during the flight. All in all, I enjoyed the respite from the directorial hunt.

The Mirisches offered me a picture to edit when I got home—an Elvis movie—but, donkey that I was, I had a director's chair in mind. However, it was all to no avail. I had no luck. I needed to get smart and stop this quest, but I remained stubborn. Then fate and my daughter Judy stepped in.

Chapter 14

One day in 1962, Judy said to me, "My friend Nancy, Marty Jurow's daughter, told me her dad wants to meet you. I've invited him to come up here Sunday afternoon. Be cleaned up and shaved."

Jurow, a tiny man physically, was a giant in the world of film agentry. An officer in a big agency in Hollywood, he had now become a motion picture producer. We met, we chatted. I liked him, he liked me. We talked about everything in the world and not one word about movies. I wondered what this was all about. I found out the next day when he called.

"Ralph, I'm going to produce a picture in Rome titled *The Pink Panther*. Blake Edwards is the director. We want you to edit the film and we will not talk to anyone else until you decide whether you will do it or not."

I was very flattered! At this time, Edwards was the hottest director in town, having just done *Breakfast at Tiffany's* and *Days of Wine and Roses*.

"If you decide to do it," Jurow continued, "go over to the Mirisches, who will be the producing company, and make your deal. We start shooting in Rome in one month."

This was a pretty exciting conversation. Back to Rome? My wife, Teddy, and I loved and knew Rome after *Quo Vadis* and *Ben-Hur*. And it was a chance to work again for the Mirisch Company, a swell bunch of people.

After a year of floundering, I needed to earn some money. I guess I had to forget about being a director and get back to work. I made the deal and took the job. I was at peace with myself. I knew I could make a contribution to any picture I worked on.

I now set about selling Ralph Winters to Blake Edwards. Blake was not tall, though a very handsome man, with a ruddy complexion, curly brown hair, and charisma galore. He could charm you out of your eyeteeth and make you beg him to take them. He did four movies for the Mirisches, all of which I cut, and we developed a great relationship. In a way, I was launched on a new career. *The Pink Panther* turned out to be the most pleasant picture to work on thus far in my career.

The Hotel De La Ville on via Sistina at the top of the Spanish Steps in Rome was home for Teddy and me. Via Sistina empties into Piazza Bernini. Right at the bottom of via Sistina was a little café that we wandered into the first night we were in Rome. It had about six tables. We had a delicious meal and were waited on by a man named Alberto with whom we became acquainted. A warm friendship developed between us. He was short and chubby and a barrel of laughs. He spoke about four words of English. On the wall was a single piece of art—an American calendar opened to the month of November that displayed a picture of the San Francisco skyline. He was always teasing us about San Francisco being a nicer place than Los Angeles. He seemed to know about the competition between the two cities. How he found out about this bit of trivia, I'll never know.

We were invited to his home for dinner one Sunday. It was raining very heavily and when we arrived, here was this little guy standing at the bus stop waiting for us in the driving rain. I visited him every time we went back to Rome. On my last trip, I was saddened to learn that he was dead.

Panther was really great to work on. Lots of laughs, no night work, and plenty of good times in the city. Pretty soon the company went to Cortina, a resort north of Rome, to shoot a sequence in the snow. They were gone for four days. When they got back, Blake told me that he was worried about the sequence and wanted to look at it when I got it together. How refreshing. Not "how fast can you show it to me" but "when." I was really beginning to like this guy. "If necessary, we will go back to Cortina and reshoot," he said.

Blake's mechanics were quite simple and his film was not too tough to put together. I massaged the material for four days. Skiing sequences are usually shot silently. After the sequence was cut, it certainly seemed to need sound to help sell it. I laid a piece of old Henry Mancini music on top of the cut material. This music could only be used temporarily. Each picture has to have its own score, but for editorial or preview purposes, you can use anything.

Now I was ready.

I went to the set and told Blake the Cortina scene was ready. Up he came to the projection room with his entourage. The film started. On came the sequence with Mancini's great music, which really made the sequence sound good and look good. I was watching Blake out of the corner of my eye. He absolutely levitated. Bingo! I had him. After the film stopped, he said he didn't think retakes were necessary and he was very pleased. I walked onto the set later in the day and he greeted me within earshot of the whole company. "Ralph, you can put music on my cut stuff anytime you want to."

Thus started a fantastic relationship that would lead to thirteen movies over the next twenty years, including *The Pink Panther, A Shot in the Dark, The Party,* and *What Did You Do in the War, Daddy?*

I will always have a soft spot in my heart for *The Pink Panther* because it was the picture that launched me with the Mirisches and Blake Edwards.

One confession before we leave *Panther.* There is a cut in the picture that drives me crazy. David Niven is in Inspector Clouseau's bedroom where he should not be. He is hiding behind a drape, between the drape and a window. Just when he thinks the coast is clear and starts to step out from behind the drape, a maid opens the door to the room and steps in. He jumps back behind the drape. Their actions happen simultaneously. If I had shown the maid first, Niven would have been delayed and if I had shown Niven first the maid becomes delayed.

I changed it every which way I could think of, but it never looked good, and to this day it doesn't look good. Every time I look at this spot in the picture, I cringe. Funnily enough, a few years later, I saw the sequence and had an idea how to recut it and make it look better—I think. If I could get my hands on the film again, I would take another crack at it. El Donko.

Chapter 15

How a talented guy like Blake Edwards got stuck in a bad movie deal like *Soldier in the Rain,* I'll never know. Ralph Nelson, the director, was just not the right man to direct a delicate story with lots of mood like this one. Blake wrote the script and he should have directed it, but he made some cockamamie deal that gave Paramount power over the script and required Blake to be the producer. If Blake had directed this turkey, maybe something good might have come out of it.

Anyway, I got pulled in, too. By this time, my relationship with Blake was in full flower and I wanted to keep it that way. I wasn't very happy, but I jumped in with both feet. I liked all the directors I worked with except a very few. Ralph Nelson, the director on this film, was among the very few. He was a pure journeyman and just not a nice guy. In addition, the movie starred Jackie Gleason and Steve McQueen, big television names, and I think Nelson was afraid of both of them.

Blake got ahold of me the day before the picture started shooting and said, "Watch this guy and see that he shoots a nice picture and gets all the angles you need."

I was down on the set the first day of shooting all bright-eyed and bushy-tailed. I sidled up to Nelson and said, "I'm here to help you in any way you see fit to use me."

Nelson looked at me and said "Sure, kid, just give me a few minutes to get this scene, and we'll chat." But he never came near me. I hung around all day. Nada!

Next day I was on the set again. "Good morning, Mr. Nelson."

"Mornin', kid." Some kid! I was fifty-four years old.

73

Again, I hung around all day. Niente! I began to have a hunch, just slightly, that I was being ignored. On the third morning, I went to the cutting room and started cutting on the first two days' dailies. To hell with trying to help Nelson. Blake looked at the first two days' work and then disappeared. I never went near the set again. I didn't think Mr. Nelson missed me, but my turn was coming.

Finally, this great epic finished shooting and Nelson and I met in the screening room to work on the picture. After one of the scenes went by on the screen, he stopped the film and said, "That's pretty good, but we'll work on it some more when we get into the cutting room."

I said, "What do you mean 'we'? You're not coming into the cutting room. Just tell me what you want and I will cut the picture anyway you wish, but I can't work with you hanging over my shoulder." On this happy note, we broke for lunch. I went upstairs to the cutting room, and by the time I got there, the phone was ringing. It was Blake.

"Meet me in the commissary," he said, "and bring the script."

During lunch, Blake and I went through the script and just cut the hell out of the picture on paper. "Make these changes in the film," Blake said.

"Gee, Blake, what am I going to tell this guy when he wants to make changes? There's no point in discussing the cutting on stuff that's coming out of the picture anyway."

"Just tell him that I had a couple of ideas I wanted you to try."

"And if he wants to know what the ideas are?" I asked.

"Well, just say I didn't want him to have any preconceived ideas."

Sure enough, I went back to the screening room after lunch and told Nelson the story and he asked me what the cuts would be. When I told him what Blake said to tell him, Nelson got a weird look on his face. I was really embarrassed. The guy was entitled to the director's cut anyway, but he never said a word. He just left the screening room, and to this day, I never saw or heard from him again.

It was not nice of Blake to handle things this way, but Ralph Nelson was not a nice guy. Blake and I finished the picture without Nelson. Though it was selfish, I was glad to be rid of him.

In the fall of 1963, Blake Edwards called me while we were still working on *Soldier in the Rain* to say he was going to London to do *A Shot in the Dark* for the Mirisches. Blake had never worked in London and he wanted me to go along. "I'm afraid of those limeys and I don't want to be over there alone without you."

This was to be an Eady Plan picture, which allowed American producers to come to England to make movies with American money; however, they had to use all-English crews. If the producers then qualified for Eady, their take would come right off the first dollar the pictures earned in England. Actors and directors were exempt, but editors were not.

"I'd be glad to go," I told him, "but their unions are very strong, and they'll never let me in. I think we'll have to forget it."

"I'm doing the Mirisches a favor by doing this picture," Blake said. "They can do one for me and work this out." The picture had been abandoned by the director Anatole Litvak, and the Mirisches were high and dry. They also had other time commitments on the movie, and starting dates with other actors to be considered.

Work it out they did. Ray Kurtzman, the Mirisches' young, short but mighty, in-house lawyer, got on his horse and fixed the problem. He discovered that you could work in England if their union could not furnish certain kinds of manpower. Since they did not employ supervising editors, I was brought in under that title. I thought this was silly, but it got me in.

I stayed on the set for most of the shoot, which meant one more body to watch out for. In fact, my presence caused a problem the day they were shooting a very difficult set-up in which the camera swung wildly in a big long angle and came to a stop only when the scene ended.

When Blake questioned the cameraman as to how it looked, he said, "It was fine. Except Ralph was caught in the last few seconds of the shot." Unfortunately, I was right on the edge of the set. This meant the take was no good and would have to be reshot.

"Put a lamp shade on Ralph's head," Blake said calmly, "and let's reshoot the scene." It broke everyone in the crew up and saved me an embarrassing moment.

The English editor on the picture, Bert Bates, resented my being there— in the extreme. The bastard paid no attention to me whatever. Whenever I made a cutting suggestion, or even asked him to make a change, he charmingly acquiesced. Then he did nothing. He made my life miserable.

When the picture finished shooting, Blake went home and left me in London to work on the picture and also to go to Paris and reshoot some shots of an ambulance, which I did.

Then there was a sequence that took place in a nightclub with flamenco dancing that I felt needed to be recut. When I asked Bates to do the work, he said, "Go ahead. You recut it."

Afraid that just putting my hands on the film might jeopardize the Eady Plan, I said, "You know the union won't allow this."

"I am the union," Bates sneered.

"Well, if that's the case, I'll do it." So, I recut the sequence, and luckily, we got away with it. Also luckily, it was soon decided that we should bring the picture back to Hollywood for final editing. I was delighted to get home and get away from Bert. But not so fast, my lovely. Since they could not afford to endanger the Eady Plan, Bert was brought over to the States.

Even worse, Al Wood, who was the head of the production department for the Mirisch company, asked me to go to the airport in L.A. and pick Bates up.

"Nothing doing," I said. "I don't like that guy." I'll get even with that limey, I muttered under my breath. He's in my territory now.

"You'll go down to the airport and pick him up because you're the only one who knows what he looks like."

I screamed and hollered but I was stuck. Bert and I never exchanged two words all the way back to town.

We had to set up cutting rooms in a motel in Hollywood since we were not allowed to bring Eady Plan film into any studio. I brought some books in to try to get Bert distracted. It was March and the weather happened to be beautiful. Bert sunned himself at the pool and read the books while I cut the picture to my heart's content.

Gradually, ever so gradually, we started to communicate with one another. At last, I invited him to my home for dinner.

One day I said to Bert, "What did you think when you saw me at the airport?"

"I was never so glad to see anybody in my whole life as I was to see you," he said. Well, that floored me. And before you knew it, we became fast friends. In fact, he turned out to be a swell guy. Or maybe he was a swell guy all along—and it was I who was the jerk.

We finished the picture—one of Blake's best—in peace.

Chapter 16

In 1965, I was elected by acclamation to the presidency of the film editors' union. I felt very honored and excited. I had turned fifty-six that year, and was very proud of myself, but with this responsibility came conflict.

The Mirisches were making a picture, *Cast a Giant Shadow,* in Europe. Gene Ruggiero, a very close friend of mine, was their editor on the picture. Gene and I had come to MGM together in 1928. He was a great golfer and we had played together many times. We were buddies. Often, we would meet at six A.M., play eighteen holes of golf and be at work by nine A.M. Through the years we bummed around together but, as we got older we saw less and less of each other, especially since we were both gone from MGM.

Soon after I took office as president of the film editors' union, Marvin Mirisch called to tell me that they were very unhappy with Gene's work on *Shadow.* They wanted to take him off the picture. As president and representative of the union, I had to give permission to replace Gene. Now, Gene was a fine editor who had among his many credits the award-winning *Ninotchka.* To complicate matters, they wanted to replace him with Bert Bates, the English editor who was also now my very good friend.

I was sick about having to make this decision. On the one hand, I loved the Mirisches and wanted them to have whatever they felt was best for them. In addition, I could not upset the delicacy of our relationship with the English unions, which at this point was beginning to thaw. On the other hand, I knew it would jeopardize my friendship with Gene. Of course, I made the right business decision, but Gene would not speak to me for years. Eventually, he came around . . . a little, but this experience cast a cloud over my term of office.

What helped take the sting out of that year was working on *The Great*

Race. This was just a big cartoon-like picture and a lot of fun to work on, especially with Tony Curtis as "The Great Leslie" and Jack Lemmon as "Professor Fate."

The company had a second unit just for shooting chases and stunts. After Blake watched the first couple of days' work, however, he fired the second-unit director and decided that I should shoot the second unit.

Although I had no time to prepare, I was excited about the chance. I promoted my assistant editor to editor to keep the cutting going, and plunged in. On my first day as a second-unit director, I had to shoot Professor Fate jumping out of a second-story window, expecting to land on his car. The car has a trampoline on top of it. Just as he jumps, the car pulls away and the professor falls into an open manhole. Of course, no one can fall out of a second story window directly into a manhole. Therefore, the shot had to be filmed backwards, pulling the stunt man out of the hole and up in the air and through the window while reversing the film in the camera. Making stunts like this one work on film was fun and kept me out of the cutting room for nine weeks.

Blake always went first cabin and he arranged for us to do the same. Wherever we traveled, it was first-class transportation, accommodations, and restaurants—always the best.

During this time, we traveled to Paris, Vienna, Salzburg, and as always, we went first class. Not everything went smoothly, and I still had lots to learn. While in Vienna, I shot a scene in the courtyard of a castle that disappointed Blake when he saw the dailies. I felt terrible, but he told me not to be upset. This man always took things in stride. The good and the bad. He decided to build a courtyard in the studio at home and reshoot. He must have realized the sequence itself could be better because he proceeded to rewrite it—and make it better at home under better control. And it was.

No one is supposed to look at cut material before the director or producer looks at it. I was working on a sequence that deals with Jack Lemmon (Professor Fate) getting stuck in his car on the banks of the Lena River. I had the sequence cut together and was running it in a projection room when Jack Lemmon happened to walk by. Hearing the sound coming out of the projection booth, he came into the room and watched the sequence with me. I was worried about Jack being in there but I was not about to throw him out. He loved the sequence and ran down to the set to tell Blake about it. Now I *was* worried. Up came Blake and wanted to take a look-see. Instead of getting upset about Jack seeing it, he complimented me very highly on the cut.

There was a pie fight in the picture, which was fashioned after the pie fight in a Laurel and Hardy movie. It took place in the royal bakery. By the time the sequence was over, everyone in the scene was to be completely inundated with pies. While all these pies were flying around, Tony Curtis, as the Great Leslie, was supposed to walk through without getting any pie on him, until the last moment, when he gets it right in the kisser.

The progression of the pie throwing had to be cut very carefully, as you could not show an actor with pie on his face one minute, then cut back to a close-up of the same face with a little less pie on it. In the end, we were able to create a sequence where everyone is bombarded with pies while Tony walks through without one bit of pie having hit him.

I must confess, he did have one tiny speck of pie on him, but I was the only one who saw it, and I never said a word . . . til now.

Chapter 17

In 1968, Marvin Mirisch called to ask if I would be available to help out on the cutting of *The Thomas Crown Affair*. I wasn't working at the time and was delighted to work on the picture with Hal Ashby, who was the editor of record. Hal had won an Oscar for editing *In the Heat of the Night*. Also, Norman Jewison, the director, already had to his credit quality pictures like *The Russians Are Coming, The Russians Are Coming* and *In the Heat of the Night*, which had also won an Academy Award for best picture. I considered these two fellows pretty good company.

The picture was really in the late stages of editing and I sort of took it over for Hal, who was moving on to become Norman's assistant. They handed me a chess sequence to cut, where Steve McQueen and Faye Dunaway were the players. It was a very suggestive and sexy scene filled with innuendo and all kinds of nuances.

After I cut it together, both Norman and Hal were so happy with the result that both insisted that I share screen credit for editing. I told them I hadn't done enough work on the movie to earn a credit, but they wouldn't have it any other way. I really tried to talk them out of it, but they persisted. That's why I always look at my credit on *The Thomas Crown Affair* with a jaundiced eye. However, my work on that picture earned me the assignment on Jewison's next picture, *Gaily Gaily*.

In the meantime, I was fifty-nine years old and had just become a grandpa for the first time. His name is Christopher. Whatever had happened to that sweet, naive, eighteen-year-old boy named Ralphie?

Gaily Gaily, a film I cut in 1969, was a tough, tough movie. Looking back, I think some of my own doing made this picture a tough assignment for me.

Norman Jewison, the director, not a big man physically, was a good-looking guy in his forties, with a nice physique and brown hair that was graying at the temples. He was very talented, and as I've said, his record is sensational. Now that I was on one of his movies, as the editor on my own, I really wanted to please him and I tried like hell to ingratiate myself with him.

I turned sixty on this picture—climbin' up there. Norman's secretary sent me a birthday card, that said "Happy birthday to a nice man." Normie had inserted the word "old" before "man." I did not care too much for the joke but nevertheless, I liked him and I think he liked me but somehow—and for some reason I could not put my finger on—we just did not click together.

After the picture was finished, I thought of a couple of possible reasons why that might be so. Hal Ashby was Norman's favorite editor and he was the greatest. Now promoted to be Norman's assistant, Hal was soon to become a well-respected director as well. It was a tough act for me to follow. In addition, although I said earlier that I learned not to argue with a director, I think I forgot my lesson on this one.

There is a sequence where Melina Mercouri is giving a party in her home and singing a song to her guests. I thought the cutting on this number should be casual, and not cutting on the beat of the music, the way a song in a musical picture would be cut. I felt it needed a kind of flow that would let the cutting come where the scene led it and the music would follow. I showed it to Norman that way, but he thought the song should be cut on the beat. We argued the point. Naturally, I showed it to him, cut the way he wanted to see it. And that's the way it stayed. I still think the way I showed it to him first was better.

Since I wrote that last sentence, I've looked at that sequence again and I must say in all honesty that cutting it the way Jewison wanted it looked pretty darned good—much better than the way I first cut it. Hmmm!

There was another problem around a scene where a hearse pulled in behind a funeral parlor. Norman took a lot of time to set up a shot where the camera is shooting straight down from a height onto the action. It was a beautiful piece of film, but, try as I might, I could not get it to look good in the cutting, and I took it out.

I knew they'd had a rough time making the shot. I should have left it in the picture, but, donkey that I am, I did not. Of course, when Norman saw the cut sequence he raised hell because the shot was not in the picture. I put the shot into the picture. When he saw it, he, too, knew that it did not work.

He said, "It doesn't work. Take it out."

It was a hollow victory for me because I was wrong not to keep the shot in the picture in the first place.

When Norman finished a day's shooting he would come up to his office with his entourage, relax, have a drink, and generally unwind. This was great except he never looked at his dailies until quite late. I rarely left the studio before nine-thirty, and I hated it.

Norman shot a lot of film and it was tricky stuff. After he finished the picture, it took me nine weeks to get it all together. That's a disgraceful amount of time to keep the director waiting to see his movie. There was a tremendous amount of film to go through, but that's no excuse. A good editor gears himself to work fast when it becomes necessary. Norman was fine about it. Walter Mirisch was fine about it. I don't know why it took so long. It just did.

You know, the word "argument" is quite ambiguous, and there are all kinds of ways to argue one's point. I don't think I handled myself too well on *Gaily Gaily*—I just ran a bad race.

In the end, the picture was not successful. A well-made movie, it just did not do any business. I think one of the problems could have been casting.

After *Gaily* was finished, Norman was going to go to London to prepare his next movie, *Fiddler on the Roof*. I was dying to do that movie, and I'm sure Norman knew I wanted to do it, but I was never asked, and I would never ask him about it. Walter Mirisch wanted me to do it, too, but he never told me to ask, for which I was eternally grateful. I did not want to create the possibility of an embarrassing moment, and I did not want to hear a "no."

I never did find out why he didn't ask me to be the editor and I grieved about it for a long time.

In the meantime, I was sixty years old and I had just become a grandpa for the second time. Her name is Nancy. Gosh!

Chapter 18

For *most* of my career, I had good relationships with both producers and directors. During my years at MGM, while the major studios were in flower, I think one could say that the producer was the "boss." He was, for the most part, the creative head of the picture. He was an employee of the studio. He did not have to worry about money to make the picture. He assigned the director and usually had creative autonomy. The director was also an employee of the studio and—for the most part—bowed to the wishes of the producer. Of course, there were exceptions. Autonomy also depended on the deal made by any outside director if he came in on a one-picture deal with the studio.

As the Directors Guild became stronger through the years, the director earned the right of "first cut," then the right of one preview, then the right of two previews. Gradually, over the years, the director's input became the guiding factor in the cutting of the picture.

I always tried to ingratiate myself with the people for whom I worked without being obsequious, and to be as honest as I could in my opinions and ideas, no matter with whom they happened to agree or disagree. Certain likes and dislikes were bound to occur anyway in a highly volatile business. When I first started to edit, a friend said to me, "Remember, when they like you, your mistakes are laughs. When they don't like you, you can't do anything right."

How true! How true!

In 1970, *The Hawaiians* was to be personally produced by Walter Mirisch, to be directed by Tom Gries, and to be shot entirely in Hawaii. Walter wanted me to edit, but I was still working on *Gaily* for Norman Jewison. Besides, I had been traveling a lot and frankly did not want to go to Hawaii at that time. I resisted.

Walter said, "You don't have to stay there. Just come over and have some conversations with Gries and look at whatever dailies there are. Then you can go back and do the editing at home."

I liked working for the Mirisches. Walter and I were fast becoming blood brothers and, in the end, I agreed to go. Anyway, I had nothing else in the works after *Gaily*. Since I was not quite finished with Jewison's picture when *The Hawaiians* started shooting, the dailies started to pile up. Once I finished cutting *Gaily,* Walter and I dashed over to Hawaii with an armload of film.

Unbeknownst to me, Walter had arranged to have all the cutting equipment sent to Hawaii. When I got there and found out that the cutting room was all set up, I was upset—for about twenty seconds. I was really flattered. Walter knew he had me in his hip pocket and that he could talk me into staying there for the duration of the shooting. It was tough to get mad at this guy. Besides, the company was shooting on the beach on Maui.

I decided that life was not so bad after all. Hey! Hawaii was a nice place. I sent for my wife and settled down to a sojourn in Hawaii with steak and Maui onions.

I had met Tom Gries, the director, stateside. I remembered him to be a fine-looking man, muscular, about six feet tall, and he seemed to be a decent fellow. We went directly to the set where I got a lukewarm "hello" from Gries. I knew what was bothering him. I was the producer's "baby." I thought, "Hell, here we go again."

I never could understand a director's negative reaction when he had an editor who had a good relationship with the producer. To a man, they always seemed to resent it, when in fact they should have been pleased. After all, the editor can keep peace in the family and occasionally smooth ruffled feathers.

Now, Blake Edwards couldn't have cared less. In fact, Walter Mirisch and I were walking down the studio street one day tête-à-tête and Blake happened to be walking by. Big smiles and greetings. Blake never asked me what our conversation was about. He never mentioned it to me.

I chose to overlook Tom Gries' pique, even when he told me, "I don't want anyone to see my dailies before I see them." Many directors feel this way, as they like to look at their film before the producer or anyone else looks. But with Walter ensconced here in Hawaii, it would have been pretty hard to hide the film. The editor was in the middle again.

I said, "Tom, I don't think it's my place to refuse to show dailies to the producer before you see them, if he so requests."

Tom hesitated a bit, then said, "Well, I don't want him to look at any cut stuff before I do."

"I'm sorry," I said, "but I can't refuse to show the film to the producer. If you don't want Walter to look at your film before you do, then you tell him."

Of course, Tom never said a word to Walter. And, of course, whenever the film came in, Walter did look at it. I tended strictly to business and eventually Tom warmed up. As the weeks went by, we got along fine and we got a good movie. Tom Gries was not without talent, and I think he did a fine job of directing this movie.

Chapter 19

The All-American Boy, a real doozy, told the story of a broken-down boxer who comes back to his home town. Jon Voight, a very pleasant guy and an Oscar-winning actor, had the starring role, but even he couldn't bail this movie out.

Because I needed the work, and not knowing what I was in for, I took the assignment. *Jupiter's Darling* was not a very good movie, but *The All-American Boy* was the champion dog of all time.

The picture had three main problems: the producer, the executive producer, and the director. Joe Naar, the producer, was not too distinguished physically. Let's just say he wouldn't have made Cary Grant worry. Formerly an agent, Joe had never produced a picture before. The executive producer, a nice, bland, white-haired gentleman by the name of Saul Krugman, was also a former agent, and he had never executive-produced a picture before. The third guy in this triumvirate was the writer-director, Charles Eastman, a tall, fair-haired man, not quite obese, but quite rude, who had never directed a picture before.

Oy vey! I thought. What have I gotten myself into? I'll never know how Warner Bros. bought into this one. Jack Warner must have been spinning in his grave. At least the cameraman, Phil Lathrop, a very good friend of mine, who was also good at his craft, was working on the picture.

The company flew to San Francisco to start shooting. I went along to help Charles Eastman see that we had the appropriate coverage; this meant making sure the director had the proper angles so the picture could be cut together. Nightmare time. After about ten days, this joker decided he knew all about camera angles, and there was no need for me to stay.

Was I glad to get out of there. I came home and started to cut the film. In my entire career, I truly cannot remember when it was so tough to put anything together. Every cut I made was a fight.

Finally, after three months, this turkey finished shooting, and then the fun began. Eastman decided to come into the cutting room to help me. Dear God! My cutting room was just a cubbyhole, maybe the size of a large desk. Eastman had a black German shepherd dog that went everywhere with him. When Blackie lay down there wasn't much room left in this tiny place. The dog understood everything Charlie said to him. I am not kidding. One day on the set, Eastman said to Blackie, "Get in the car." I watched as the dog jumped through a window into the car. Here was a force to be reckoned with. I think Blackie would have made a great executive at Warner Bros.

The three of us sat down to work on the picture. I gave the dog the best seat. I gave Eastman the next-best seat—I didn't want him to tell Blackie to bite me. We started on a sequence that I had fought to get together. As I remember now, I lost the fight. The sequence was running about three minutes. After two days of recutting it for Charlie and Blackie, it ran five minutes in length. I was now about ready to kill him, the dog, and myself. At the rate Chuck was going, this movie was going to run about five hours, and with a tremendous amount of film left to be put together, it was going to take months to finish this piece of junk.

Frontal nudity had just become very popular at this time (not that it never was) and Chuckie-boy shot a sequence where the leading lady in this piece is stripped to the waist. The poor thing looked terrible with bared breasts—they looked like a couple of empty wallets. I said to this great and erudite director, "Charles, you can't use that shot of the girl. It looks terrible."

"It's perfectly natural," the great one replied. "Many women's breasts look this way."

I was horrified and depressed. Up to now, I had never walked out on a picture, and though I really wanted to, I decided not to take a walk on this one.

While having a smoke, I ran into Saul Krugman, my brilliant executive producer. He said "Ralph, we want to get the movie out in time for it to be considered for an Academy Award this year." It was already October, and the picture would have to be released in December to be considered for an award.

I thought about the scene Eastman and I had just worked on and fought to control myself. I lost the fight and burst into hysterical laughter. "Saul," I said between sobs, "the only award this picture will ever be considered for is what ash can will have the honor of getting it."

He looked at me like he'd been shot. About an hour later, Rudy Fehr, my good friend and the head of the editorial department for Warner Bros., came down to see me. Rudy, a fat, stocky German refugee with a dark complexion, had fled from Germany during the Hitler regime and still spoke with an accent. His religion was Jewish, but he had the heart of a Nazi. It seems like this conversation I'd had with Saulie had gone up through the executive offices and bounced around the lot a few times. Rudy was upset with me.

"Ralph, you can't talk to an executive producer that way. It's not nice."

I said, "Rudy, if you are a good friend of mine, you'll fire me right now. Please."

The next day he came to see me again. "Ralph, we have hired another editor to help you. This is the way it's going to work. We want you to continue to edit the picture together, but Eastman will recut your editing with the new editor."

I couldn't believe my ears. Up to now, I had racked my brains, trying to figure a way to get off this turkey. This was manna from heaven, but I was still angry. "Now let me get this straight, Rudy. I am to edit this mountain of junk together while Eastie sits down with the new editor and Blackie to recut my work?"

"Yes."

"Never! If I edit, then I re-edit. I'm not going to sit in this horrible cutting room that stinks of old age and wood rot, that you and your puny bosses don't want to rebuild, while these two jokers recut my stuff."

"But that's the way they want it done, Ralph."

Who was I to argue with the momentous decisions that came from this well of brilliant executives? "I quit. And do me a personal favor, Rudy. Take my name off this fine, delicate piece of work." I then got my coat and other personal stuff and took off, running. I went right home and got drunk!

If ever a picture was raped, slain, massacred, then *The All-American Boy* takes the ten-layer cake. This horrible excuse for entertainment that was foisted on an undeserving public was done in by the writer who destroyed the director and was equally done in by the director who destroyed the writer. They deserved each other.

P.S. It took a long time for this epic to be finished. Three editors were hired and fired. I heard somewhere that this great work was in the cutting room for a year, and after maybe two or three days of release, it was pulled from the theaters. When the movie was in its final death throes, the sagacious—and I use the term loosely—Mr. Eastman decided that all the editors on the picture should be credited. After learning that my name was on the main title of this epic, I went to the nearest curb and let my blood. I'm not sure how Blackie handled it.

Chapter 20

It was 1971 and I was out of work. While scanning *Variety* for jobs, I noticed a little squib that Jack Lemmon was going to direct a movie entitled *Kotch* for ABC's motion picture arm.

I called him right away. "Jack, have you hired an editor yet?"

"Why, yes, Ralph—you."

And so I went to work with Jack on *Kotch*. This guy Lemmon, believe me, is a credit to the human race. The picture was shot in Palm Springs and I spent the first ten days of shooting down there with this sweet, wonderful man. He was always nice and even-tempered, even though this movie was Jack's first and, so far, only directorial effort.

One sequence was shot on the Palm Springs Tramway, in the San Jacinto Mountains. I had and still have a terrible case of acrophobia—I just cannot stand heights. I rode up and down in this thing all day, nervous as a cat while the sequence was being shot. But by the end of the shooting day, I could have been hung out the window and it would not have bothered me. However, as soon as we finished the sequence, the old acrophobia came back over me like a blanket.

This movie was a piece of fluff, but enjoyable to work on and enjoyable for the audience. Walter Matthau and Debra Winters (no relation) were the leads. In a sequence that came late in the picture, Debra Winters, who is pregnant, and Matthau are racing down the mountain in a rickety old car. Her labor pains are coming pretty rapidly and it's getting dark. They have to stop at a filling station where Kotch delivers the baby in the confines of the public bathroom.

There were three angles in this sequence: a close-up of Walter, a close-up of Debra, and a full shot that was angled behind Walter's back. By cutting back and forth, we were able to generate some good suspense in this sequence. Maybe that scene was what earned the picture a nomination for an Oscar for best editing. I was surprised and delighted, though I knew it didn't have a chance to win. At the Academy Awards, I just sat back and enjoyed the show.

In the meantime, my second grandson, Zachary, was born. Let me see, I was now sixty-two years old and I had three grandchildren. Gettin' up there!

Chapter 21

By 1972, I had cut nine pictures for the Mirisch Company. Our relationship was terrific, and I was very happy working for them. At this time, Walter talked to me about editing *Avanti,* which they were preparing to shoot in Rome. It starred Jack Lemmon and was to be directed by the great Billy Wilder, who had made such wonderful movies as *Some Like It Hot, The Apartment, Witness for the Prosecution,* and others that became great classics.

"Walter, I don't know this man," I said. "I would find it very hard to walk up to him and ask him about cutting his picture. You ask him."

"No," he said, "you can do it." And we continued to argue about it without any conclusion.

One day while walking on the lot, I spied Wilder sitting on the front seat of his car talking to Norman Panama, a writer and producer, who was an old friend of mine from our MGM days. I went over to say hello and Norman introduced me to Wilder. Norman also complimented me on my work in front of Wilder.

Only of medium height, Billy Wilder was an imposing figure, quick of step and quick of tongue. He had a round face and brown eyes and always wore sport shirts with button-down collars open at the throat, and a peaked cap that hid his partially bald head. He had an aura about him that was magnetic, charismatic.

I'm thinking, it's now or never. I screwed up my courage, took a deep breath, and said, "Mr. Wilder, if you have not yet assigned an editor to *Avanti,* I would like to be considered."

He invited me to his office for a chat, and bingo! He hired me to edit the picture. Here was a man who had fled Germany during the Hitler regime.

He couldn't speak a word of English when he arrived, yet he was a writer. Now he spoke English with perfect grammar but a slight accent, and pronounced my name "Raulf."

I was not working at this time and Teddy and I decided to go over to Europe ten days before the picture started. We started off in Amsterdam, rented a car, and drove through Holland, Belgium, Germany, Switzerland, and into Italy. We gave up the car in Florence and took the Rapido into Rome, arriving a few days before the start of shooting. It gave us a chance to get reacquainted with Rome. I was sixty-three and I felt great—ready to charge into this new project.

The company was shooting in a little studio, Safa Palatino, almost around the corner from the Coliseum. It boasted only two stages, but had a lovely, intimate feel to it. I could step out of my cutting room and there was the Coliseum looming up right in front of me. I loved the ambience of this tiny studio and I loved working there. And, it was spring, a great time of the year in Italy.

I did not know Wilder very well and naturally I was nervous. After the first two weeks of shooting, I wanted him to look at some cut stuff. I had about ten minutes cut together, so I said, "Billy, you ought to look at some of the film I have cut together to make sure it's all right and you don't need to reshoot anything."

He assured me he would take a look, but he didn't. I think he was superstitious and didn't want to see any edited film until the picture was finally together. However, a week or so after this conversation, he called and asked me to show him the cut sequence of our leading lady riding in the park in a Carrozza. Billy thought the photography of the girl's close-ups could be improved, and he was thinking of retaking them. In this sequence, the girl is enjoying the park, the horse bobbing along with tinkling bells on his head, the great Roman climate, and the ride in the little carriage. The little horse and carriage pass an open bar where people are sitting outside the bar and having a drink. As the camera pans across this group, there is a lady nursing a baby at the very end of the pan, the gag being that everyone is having a drink in the warm summer sunshine, even the baby.

Do you believe that I cut away from the shot before the camera finished its pan past the end of the bar, missing the gag completely? Well, I did. Billy just about fainted. "Raulf!" he shouted. "How could do that? You cut off the joke!"

I blushed with embarrassment and sputtered that I would have it fixed before he could get back to the set. Here I was trying to impress the man with my "great" editing and I really blew it. The simplest kind of a scene to cut. Waiting all these weeks to show him some of my work and I make a blunder like that. It felt like someone hit me over the head with a baseball bat.

I stepped onto the set after lunch, and from clear across the set I heard, "Raulf, how could you do that?" I slunk back to the cutting room.

The next morning, as was my habit every morning, I beat him down to the set. Whenever possible, I liked to be on the set to be there just in case he wanted me for something and to greet him. I'm sure no editor he ever had was down on the set every morning to greet him when he arrived. I loved to beat him in every morning, anyway. I was slowly ingratiating myself with him. And now this silly error.

As soon as he came in, I said, "Good morning, Billy." And he said without batting an eye, "Raulf, how could you do that?"

Now I figure I'm dead. How am I going to get this guy, this wonderful guy that I am falling in love with, off my back. I said "Billy, I just must be a complete idiot."

He looked at me and without the blink of an eye said, "Then nothing more need be said." And he never mentioned it again.

Ironically, the sequence died at a sneak preview. While I'm not defending myself (it was a stupid thing that I did), the mother and babe were too low on the screen so the audience's eyes never went to them, as mine never had. The picture was too long anyway, and the sequence should have been taken out of the picture. It's still in.

In any case, Wilder and I really developed a great relationship. I loved that man. He was very fair and had a marvelous sense of humor.

When Billy was shooting another sequence in Sorrento, I brought some dailies over from Rome to show him and stayed over for a few days. He bought me a little straw hat with a colorful ribbon that I still have. He was shooting a night sequence where the Trotter brothers, characters in the picture, were playing a scene standing in a circle. One of them speaks a funny line, we hope, but he is standing with his back to the camera. I suggested to Billy that he shoot a CU so we could see the actor's face. Billy didn't think it was necessary. I tried to convince him, but no soap. However, he followed me around for the next half hour, trying to convince me that we did not need the close-up. I was flattered. But I never gave in, he never shot the close-up, and the line never got a laugh.

When we got back to Hollywood and started the work of cutting the picture down, Billy and I used to brown bag it for lunch. We would meet in his office to eat and gab—memorable sessions that were full of laughs.

One day, as I opened my bag and pulled out a sandwich, Billy asked, "Raulf, is that white bread?"

"Yes."

"Eating white bread," he said, "is like dancing with your sister."

This man was a delight. Even now as I write, I can hear his voice.

These few tidbits and the puny arguments that we had are just tiny spots of paint on the great canvas that is Billy Wilder.

In 1973, I found myself working for Billy Wilder again, this time on *The Front Page.* In those days, when it was considered normal for directors to print two to three thousand feet of dailies a day, Billy printed around five hundred feet of film.

Billy liked to—what we call—camera cut. He would stage and shoot a scene to a certain point in the dialogue, overlap a few lines of that dialogue onto the next shot, then shoot the continuation.

Of, say, five hundred feet of dailies, there could be four hundred usable feet to cut into the picture. What a joy for the editor. On *The Front Page,* Wilder printed about thirty-five thousand feet for the entire picture, a very small amount of print on a feature picture. We had a big cutting room and all the film cans could fit into one corner.

But he hated close-ups. They happen to create more work for editors, too. One day, while waiting for dailies, he said, "Raulf, I owe you an apology. I shot some close-ups today."

"Don't apologize, Billy, I can use them." And when I looked at the dailies, I saw they were not close-ups at all, but more like close shots.

Izzy Diamond, who collaborated with Wilder on the script, always sat in on the cutting with Billy and me. What funny sessions they were.

I was out of there at 5 P.M. every day. As I left, I never failed to go down the corridor to visit my friend, Ferris Webster. He and I had got our breaks at about the same time at MGM. Ferris was a really fine editor and cut a lot of pictures for Clint Eastwood. At this time, he was inundated with miles of film on his movie, which kept him there until all hours.

"Good night, Ferris, old buddy, I'm just leaving and I thought I'd say good night." He screamed every epithet in the book at me as I ran down the hall.

I was on the set of *The Front Page* one day when Robert Martin, the sound man, was giving Billy holy hell about the lack of cooperation he was getting from the crew. The complaint had to do with where the mike was to be hung during the upcoming scene. From his raised dais, Martin was going up and down Billy's back in no uncertain terms.

During this tirade, Billy paced up and down in front of him, not opening his mouth. Finally, Martin stopped and Billy said, "Are you through?"

Bob said, "Yes, I'm through."

I thought, Oh boy, here it comes.

Well, Billy just turned around and walked away. Bob was right, and Billy knew it.

What a guy!

Chapter 22

When *The Spikes Gang* came along, I accepted the assignment only because I loved Walter Mirisch. I thought the script was nothing more than fair, and that's a very generous comment. The director, Richard Fleischer, was a small man, gray, hard to describe. Except for Lee Marvin, an Academy Award winner, and Ron Howard, a child star who later became a director, the cast was mostly made up of a bunch of unknown kids.

Because I was not available when this picture started, Walter decided to wait on the editing (here we go again) until I was free. I was finishing a nondescript movie at MGM titled, *The Outfit*. Meanwhile, *Spikes* was shooting in Spain, and by the time I got to work on the picture, a lot of dailies had accumulated. Walter and I looked at the material in L.A. and made up a list of about twenty-five shots that we felt were needed. We then flew to Spain and gave the list to Mr. Fleischer, requesting that these shots be made.

Finally, the picture finished shooting and we got it cut together. I don't think Fleischer and I got off to a very good start, but he was a gentleman and always very polite. However, we ran one reel at a time because Richard lost his train of thought if we stopped to talk in the middle of a reel. I thought the idea of not stopping in the middle of the reel was a good one. We ran reel one. We stopped at the end of the reel.

There is a scene in the middle of the reel where Lee Marvin is shot and his face is bleeding. I said to Richard, "That looks exactly like catsup."

"No sir, that looks exactly like blood."

"I believe the audience will think it's phony," I insisted.

"I think they will accept it," Richard said.

By now, my assistant, Frank Urioste, and my second assistant, who is now a grown-up Larry Mirisch, were making faces and dying. This was a silly argument on my part. Why did I need to get into a discussion about blood on an actor's face? My job was only to edit the film after it comes to me. Hey, it was in the film anyway, and I was sure the company was not going back to Spain to reshoot it, so I shut up. That was our discussion of reel one.

We ran reel two straight through, stopping at the end. A long dialogue sequence occurs in this reel that required a great deal of careful editing on my part. I cut it and recut and massaged it. I thought it was very good and well cut.

I asked Richard if there was anything he wanted changed in the reel and he said, "No, because it's just a straight scene. Let's go on." I worked very hard on the cutting of that scene, but he had no comment. "Just a straight scene?" Gimme a break!

During another sequence at the end of the movie, Ron Howard comes to visit Lee Marvin, who is in jail. Marvin is sitting on the edge of a cot and Howard is sitting on the floor, which is part of the scene. There is dialogue going on. However, Marvin is drunk, which was not part of the scene, and he is sitting on the cot like a hunk of stone. In fact, you could drive a Mack truck through the pauses between some of his lines.

I got rid of one of the pauses by means of a "jump cut." In most cases, when you take frames out of the middle of a scene, the action will jump, causing a disturbance to the eye—especially with a big close-up. Even taking one frame out can cause the action to jump. In this case, I jump cut sixty-four frames—four feet!—out of the middle of one of his close-ups. But Marvin was so stony, the jump was never detected.

Although Walter decided to have this scene retaken, the original, except for Marvin's pauses, was much, much, better than the retake. Drunk as he was, we kept the old scene in the picture because there was no comparison in quality.

Walter Mirisch must have had a two-picture deal with Fleischer, who had already started preparation on *Mr. Majestyk* before we finished *The Spikes Gang*. Walter wanted me to cut this picture, too, but I still had a lot of work left on *Spikes*.

"Never mind, Ralph," he said. "You have to do this picture for me." As usual, I was no match for him, so we worked it out. I had Frank Urioste, my assistant on *Spikes*, take over as editor. A few years later, Frank became the best editor in the business—my opinion, and, I think, a very qualified one. So I went to work with Fleischer. We still stopped at the end of every reel, but we got along just fine. No blood.

In *Mr. Majestyk*, there's a scene where Charles Bronson, who stars as

Majestyk, has his watermelon crop piled up on his barn floor. A gangster shoots it up. I mean he really shoots the hell out of those watermelons. This sequence, when cut together, was too long. I should have cut it down before I ever showed it to Walter. But Walter loved it and would not let me cut it down.

An editor is supposed to get after the producer and director and try to make them cut the running time of a movie down, because most movies are too long in their first cut. Sometimes an editor has to use scare tactics, like, "Hey, Mr. Producer, this picture is too long, and if we don't try to get some footage out of it, it will die in the theaters. And you certainly don't want the audiences to die of boredom. Do you? Now get your behind moving and let's sit down and get some time cut out of this turkey." Once in a while the producer will not listen; and, once in a while, he's right. Try as I might, Walter would not let me cut the sequence down. Of course, I'm not saying Walter was right. Well, I'm not saying he was wrong, either. *Mr. Majestyk* was very successful and made a lot of money. So who in the hell am I to argue with watermelons?

Chapter 23

Nineteen-seventy-four was just a bad moment in my career. I had been out of work for some months when Jack Lemmon, bless him, got me the cutting job on *The Entertainer* for seven hundred bucks a week. At this point, that was cakes and ale. I didn't look right or left. I needed the job and I grabbed it.

The Entertainer was not designed as a feature picture but as a two-hour television show with Jack in the starring role. It was produced by the Robert Stigwood Organization, an English company which, up to this point, had not burned up the world. Marvin Hamlisch coproduced and Donald Wrye, a man I had never heard of before, was the director.

Wrye was definitely in the top five worst directors I had ever worked with. This guy would get on a close-up and play the whole scene on it. He directed the camera to move all around the set while the character was moving, with the camera fixed on a close-up of the character. This he did with many angles. It was difficult to cut into these shots and once I did, I couldn't get out of them. But believe it or not, I kept my mouth shut and set to work like a beaver.

Unlike a feature-length picture, a TV show must go out exactly to the second. When they finally finished shooting, I had about eleven thousand feet of cut stuff—eleven thousand feet of blood, sweat, and tears. Really. And I still had one sequence left to edit. So now came the time for me to do some mathematics. This movie was supposed to be a two-hour show. Two hours of running time on the screen equals 10,800 feet. Taking about ten minutes away for commercials—1,800 feet—leaves only 9,000 feet of actual show-time, or one and a half hours. With one long sequence still to cut and two hours and two minutes of time already in the bag, that left at least 3,500 feet to be cut out—or close to forty minutes—a big chunk of time to take out of a TV show.

At this point, I got a call from Mr. Hamlisch. "Ralph," he said, "we've decided to make a change in editors." I was stunned. He did not explain why they were taking me off, and I would not have asked "why" if I had been horsewhipped.

After my initial shock, I said, "Do you want me to overlap your new editor for a few days?"

"That won't be necessary," Hamlisch said. "I'm sorry, Ralph. But you and I will get together on another project some day."

By now I had recovered somewhat. "Marvin, you and I will never get together on any project. You are not a producer. You are not even a good composer. You should be slicing salami in a deli." I hung up and went home. As I thought of this moment during the next few days, my remarks to Hamlisch were not necessary. For a moment of satisfaction, I probably made an enemy. Not smart.

That evening I received a phone call from Bill Reynolds, a colleague of mine who was vacationing in Hawaii. He said he had gotten a call about taking over as the editor on this picture and he asked what I wanted him to do. This was a nice gesture on Bill's part and it made me feel better. I told him, by all means, to accept the job.

To this day, I have no idea why I was taken off the show. Not one of these jokers had seen one frame of my work. During the shoot, I had had hardly any contact with Wrye. Later, I heard from several sources that Wrye went around the cutting community bragging that he had taken Ralph Winters off his show. I guess I bawled out poor Hamlisch for nothing. He must have just been a pawn, poor schmo.

Bill Reynolds did not stay on the show very long either. He moved off to greener pastures. Irving Rosenbloom, my assistant on the project, and an absolutely marvelous fellow, wound up with it. I loved the guy, but at that point in his career he couldn't cut his way out of a paper bag.

They got this show down to footage, but I say all the worst scenes were left in. I could not believe my eyes when I saw it. I promised myself I would get even with Wrye—but I didn't have to. That posterior of a horse disappeared, which is exactly what he should have done. *The Entertainer* disappeared, too. Feh!

Chapter 24

I now was floating on the Sea of Sargasso. The Mirisch Company was idle, and I had been out of work for fourteen months. I couldn't get arrested. I couldn't even get a TV show. Well, *The Entertainer,* if you want to call that stinker a TV show, came my way in the middle of this period.

At sixty-five, I was beginning to think I was through. This was the era of Nixon's resignation; the country was in turmoil and I was in my own little world of turmoil. You'd think a guy of sixty-five would be thinking of retirement. Not El Donko. The thought never even crossed my mind. Through this very trying time, Teddy stood by me solidly and our three daughters had now been launched and married.

Finally, in December 1974, I got a call to interview for a remake of *King Kong,* with Dino De Laurentiis producing and John Guillermin directing. First, I met with the production manager, Jack Grossman, a great big fellow. Sort of overpowering, but a hell of a nice guy. After a chat with me, he called John Guillermin, and asked if we could come up to meet with him in his office.

Guillermin said, "Sit tight. I'll come over to your office."

And soon he joined us. A skinny guy, dark, with very sharp features, John Guillermin reminded me of Harry Reynolds. I was very nervous—if I'd had a hat, my fingers would have been working very hard on the brim. But John was very nice and we had a great conversation.

Jack said, "John, do you want to hear about some of Ralph's credits?"

John answered "I don't want to hear about his credits. I've made up my mind. I want him."

After fourteen months of inactivity, I felt like a bride. After John left us alone, Jack asked how much salary I wanted. I would have gone to work for a box lunch and $1.95, but we agreed on $1000 a week.

I called Marian Rothman, a friend of mine who had cut Dino's last movie, and asked her how to get along with him. She told me she didn't get along with Dino at all because she refused to show him any cut material before the director saw it—by the director's orders.

That was all I needed to know. The first time Dino asked to see a cut sequence, I said "Sure. When do you want it?" His eyes wiggled and I knew just what he was thinking. From then on, I had him in my hip pocket.

I liked Dino a lot and enjoyed working for him. Though short in stature, he was very handsome and always dressed to the nines—very natty. Like Sam Zimbalist, he was a no-nonsense guy, and, like all producers, he received a nightly report on the shooting progress of the company. The minute he got word that a sequence was finished, he called to say "Raulf, show me the sequence."

"But Dino," I'd protest, "I just got the film. I haven't had time to put it together yet." As soon as I did get a sequence together, he'd pounce on me like a tiger. But he was very considerate. I ran film for him many, many times during the course of production. Even though I was on time whenever we had a date to run, he was always in the projection room waiting for me.

Once I said, "Dino, you are always here ahead of me. That's unusual for a producer."

"I never keep people waiting," he told me. "Their time is as valuable to them as mine is to me." I loved him for that.

Halfway through the shooting, I was arbitrarily given a $250-a-week raise. I'm sure Dino approved, and it was damned nice! This was a mean picture, loaded with book-work and lots of detail.

A man in an ape suit played King Kong, which meant the stockade, trees, buildings, and any place the ape was had to be of miniature size—just like doll-house furniture. This made the man-sized ape look King Kong size. At the same time, any place the people were—stockade, buildings, trees, etc.—had to be of normal size. Naturally, everything would then look exactly as it should. And whenever Kong and the people were together in the same scene, their shots had to be made separately and put together by optical printing.

For example, when the girl was in King Kong's hand and Kong was walking, her shot had to be made as a long, long shot so that she would appear small on the screen. Then, when she was optically printed onto King Kong's hand, he would look big and she would look small. In that way, the proportions would appear correct.

Many scenes in the picture had these two elements, and some shots had three elements. My task was to instruct the lab, so they would know how to line up the two pieces, one to the other, correctly before they duped them together. The action had to be synchronized. Negative film has a number printed on every foot along the edge. This number prints through onto the positive when prints are made. So if the editor who works with the positive instructs the optical people to put the number of a certain part of one piece of positive against the number of another piece of positive, and opticalizes them together, the finished dupe will then come out with the two actions together on one piece of film.

When Kong was not moving, the normal-sized girl was put into a giant hand that was built out of leather. Normal-size girl. Normal-sized Kong. This allowed for CUs of the girl to be made.

The work on this picture was definitely tough and required tremendous concentration. Always challenging. One night after we looked at dailies in the screening room, Guillermin, cameraman Richard Kline, and I viewed a cut sequence that I had gotten ready. But Guillermin did not like the way it was cut. Then he saw some photography that he thought Kline had improperly lighted. He got so upset he started kicking the seat in front of him. In fact, he kicked it so hard that it finally broke. I thought he was going to hit me.

The next morning, Guillermin called me at home and abjectly apologized. He also called Richard Kline, who was a very good friend of mine, and apologized to him.

Kline received an Academy nomination for cinematography for his work on *Kong,* and the picture won a special Academy Award for visual effects. Despite the difficulty of the work, however, the film was not even nominated for editing. *Jaws* took the honors that year for editing, and rightly so, since it was a great cutting job, but I felt *Kong* deserved at least a nomination.

Twenty-three years later, I got a phone call from John Guillermin. "Ralph," he said, "I looked at *King Kong* the other night with a friend of mine. And I had to call to tell you that you did a sensational job on the picture." That was a nice call.

While I was finishing *King Kong,* Dino De Laurentiis asked me to go to London to take over the editing on *Orca,* another of his movies. It seemed the producer, a wild Italian named Luciano Vincenzoni, was not happy with his editor on *Orca.* He had seen *Kong* and requested me.

I said, "Dino, I don't want to go over there and take over another editor's picture, or even work on the picture with him and a lot of people I don't know. Those situations can become very touchy. Besides, the holiday season is coming up and I want to be home with my family."

"The editor is leaving the picture," Dino told me. "So it will be all yours, and we need you." That got me. Shades of Walter Mirisch. I liked Dino and thought he was a swell person. I agreed to go.

More than twelve years had elapsed since the *Shot in the Dark* days when the unions had so much power. Editors were exchanged quite frequently with English and American moviemakers at this time.

However, when I got to London, I found out that the editor, John Bloom, was not quitting the picture and, of course, he resented my coming on the show. Shades of *Shot*. I certainly didn't blame Bloom for feeling that way, but he did nothing to make my life any easier and contributed nothing to the situation. For that attitude, I disliked him very much. I was quite unhappy in this new setup, but I was there for Dino and had to make the best of it.

Once again, I was stuck working in a very hostile atmosphere. To make matters worse, I soon realized this movie could only be fair, at best. Michael Anderson, the director, though not a bad guy, was weak. The whales were wonderful; the actors were not. I had to sift through thousands of feet of film of whales to try to locate good pieces. Some of the sequences had to be completely taken apart and put back into dailies form and then recut, but there really was no way to "make" this one. In any event, Bloom did not do a very good job. If he'd been any kind of a man, he would have quit the picture once I was brought on—but he stayed. At least Bert Bates, my coeditor on *Shot,* had been a man.

I finally got through this nightmare assignment and was happy to get the hell out of there. Bloom, a nothing fellow in my opinion, later won an Oscar for *Gandhi*. I found that picture terribly long and dull, and as for an achievement in editing—my, oh my.

Chapter 25

I had just turned seventy when I got the chance to work with Blake Edwards on *10*. I have to say—and I'm happy to say—that all of Blake's movies were satisfying to work on, and I can't say enough about the atmosphere Blake created. He always looked at his dailies at noon. That meant no night running, and everything was easy and pleasant both on the set and in the cutting room.

And then there was Bo Derek, the gorgeous star. One out of many nice moments on this movie came the day I met her in the parking lot and she hugged and kissed me.

Another plus was having to take the "answer print" to London to show Blake, who was there preparing for his next movie. An answer print is the first print off the cut negative. After a day's shoot, the negative is taken from the camera and developed in the lab, and then prints are made from this negative. These prints, also developed in the lab, are the dailies (positive film) which are delivered to the editor. This is the film that the editor cuts.

When the various sequences are cut together, the story begins to grow and this cut positive becomes the "work print." After the picture finishes shooting, the work print is what the editor cuts and recuts for the producer and the director until it becomes a complete movie. When it is finally okayed, it is sent to the negative cutters, who match the negative to the work print cut for cut. Then prints are made from the cut negative for release of the picture. Naturally, any amount of prints can be made. The first print off the cut negative is called the "answer print." This answer print is screened to make sure no mistakes were made in the cut negative.

Later, I had to take a tape (made from the answer print of *10*) to Gstaad,

Switzerland, where Blake and his wife, Julie Andrews, had a chalet. We discussed some new shots that had to be made to cover the nude scenes in the picture for the TV version. I spent ten delightful days there during the month of August. Then the whole entourage came back to Hollywood from Gstaad in a little plane that flew between the high peaks of the Alps. For a couple of moments during the flight, I wondered what the hell I was doing there, but we were treated like royalty. At Geneva, we transferred to a Lear jet bound for London, disembarking onto the tarmac at Heathrow right next to a 747 that was waiting for us. Although it was now night, there was an agent waiting to look at our passports as we boarded the plane and took off for home.

In a long shot shooting from the outside, we look into a window where we see two people playing with each other, and I use the term loosely. I had a call from the censors, who had now looked at the picture, telling me that the shot had to come out of the picture because the two people were fornicating. It certainly looked that way to me, too. I called Blake, who was in New York, and told him the news. He said, "For Christ's sake, they're not fornicating. They're frolicking." I called the censors back and said, "They're not fornicating. They're frolicking." "Oh," said the censor. "In that case, we'll okay it." Wheeee! This was not work. This was fun.

1979. *S.O.B.* What the hell did *S.O.B.* mean? Son of a bitch? Save Old Blue? Who knew? Who cared, really, I never knew. No one ever told me and I never asked. We were on a roll. We had just finished *10*, which turned out very good. *S.O.B.* was an original screenplay by Blake Edwards. A satire on the motion picture industry. I think Blake had it in for some of the people in our industry.

In the movie, every time a new character entered a scene, we would cut to a black and white title describing the type of person and what their work in the industry was. Some of these descriptions were very funny and satirical. After we looked at the picture with the titles in, Blake decided that they should come out. I guess he thought they were a little too rough.

Richard Mulligan played the part of a producer whose picture had just bombed. He was now producing another one he hoped would be a blockbuster. Julie Andrews, Blake's wife, played the big star, who was married to Mulligan, the producer. At the big moment in the picture, she has to bare her breasts.

We were looking at the dailies of this big scene, and I was sitting next to Blake on one side of me and Julie on the other side. The moment came along. Julie, the actress, bares one breast in the same way a magician shows a card. Flip, flop. We barely got a glimpse. Julie was not greatly endowed anyway. Blake turned to me, "What do you think, Ralph?" I quietly slipped into a coma. I dreamed I was deep in the bowels of a coal mine in Pennsylvania, hat and light on my head, face smeared with coal dust so no one could recognize me. It didn't matter. I came out of the coma. "Blake," I nervously said, "the audience is waiting through the greater part of the movie for this. I think more has to be revealed." Blake agreed, thank God. He reshot the scene, revealing a little more. I thought the moment was handled with great taste.

Chapter 26

At seventy-two, I was still acting like a youngster. What nerve! Ronald Reagan was in his second year as president of the United States and Reaganomics was dripping down pretty good. I was now a grandpa for the fifth time as Jeffrey and Michelle had been added to the team. I was a happy man.

One Sunday afternoon when I was at home chatting with Teddy and Judy, my daughter, a phone call came in from Blake Edwards. I wasn't terribly surprised since I was editing *S.O.B.* for him at the time and assumed that's what the call was about. I was wrong.

"I'm going to London to make *Victor/Victoria,*" he announced, "and I want you to go with me to edit the film. And if you won't go, then I won't do the picture."

I took this with a grain of salt. Nevertheless, I was flattered. And though I had already done nine pictures for Blake, I could foresee some serious obstacles.

"Blake, they won't let me into England. Their union is still quite strong, and unemployment is a big problem. They've got plenty of British editors who are out of work. Besides, I've got a ton of work left to do on *S.O.B.*"

"Let me worry about that," he argued. "If they won't let you into England, we'll move the entire cutting process on *Victor/Victoria* to France. We'll send the dailies to Paris and set up cutting rooms there. We'll cut the picture there—and the sound effects, too. We'll also do the mixing and dubbing there. That will cost the English quite a few jobs."

I guess he wanted me to go pretty badly, and with these strong words, he had already turned me into a quivering mass of you-know-what. Needless to say, I accepted. If there was a catch, it was slight—Blake's son, Geoffrey, was to become one of the assistant editors on the picture. Hmmmm. However, he had worked as second assistant editor on *10* and I had found him to be a very nice boy.

Of course, the English caved in. Blake had all the film on *S.O.B.* brought over to London so we could finish the editing there. We cut the sound effects, and dubbed and scored the picture—with Mancini's great music—at the London studio as well.

This time around, the English boys were wonderful to me, and *Victor/Victoria* was a delight to work on. We were ensconced at Pinewood, a lovely little studio just outside of London. An entire two-story building was devoted to making our movie. All offices, including Blake's, along with the makeup rooms, dressing rooms, and cutting rooms were assigned to the second floor. Keeping everyone close together created an efficient environment and made working a lot less cumbersome. The lower floor was dedicated as a big stage, and all our sets were built on this stage—even the street scene set. Being winter when we arrived, this arrangement made life a lot easier when the weather was inclement.

One incident I really got a kick out of occurred around a scene that takes place in a café with the stars, James Garner and Julie Andrews. Suspecting that Julie, as Victor, is really a woman, Garner takes her out to dinner and tests her "manhood" by offering her a cigar. Trying to act like a man, Julie lights the cigar and attempts to smoke it. There is dialogue throughout the scene.

Some days later, one of the English assistants came up to me on the set and asked, "Would it worry you that Julie lights the cigar twice in the same scene?"

"Worry me?" I exclaimed. "It would devastate me!" I raced up to the cutting room like a jackrabbit, wound the reel down, put the scene into the Moviola, and took a look. There I saw Julie lighting the cigar twice in the same scene.

What made me laugh was that I had already viewed the scene cut this way and had even showed it to Blake. Neither of us noticed the miscut! Academy Award winner? Hmmmm.

We had been in London since February and it was now June. All was going smoothly and we were getting a dandy movie. And after all these years with Blake, I learned what a generosity of spirit he had. One Tuesday, my brother Bernie called me to tell me that our mother was deathly ill. I asked Blake if I could go home, saying I would leave Friday night and be back in time for work on Monday.

Blake said, "Nothing doing. You go home right now."

I did get home in time to see my mother. She died on Thursday. This kindness and the lamp shade incident on *Shot* marked Blake as one of the most considerate people I have ever known. I shall never forget him.

Chapter 27

I'm 82. Gettin' up there, ole buddy. Hadn't done too much since *Victor/Victoria*. Been sittin' around playing a lot of bridge and pleasantly passing the time. Anyhoo, one morning I got a phone call from a dear friend, Bernie Balmuth.

"Ralph," he said, "you are going to be the recipient of the Career Achievement Award. It'll be given out by the American Cinema Editors at their upcoming awards show." Bernie was chairman of the awards committee. I was thrilled to get this news.

This award, which is given out by one's peers and colleagues, is very special and an honor in every sense of the word. I found myself getting very excited.

"Who would you like to have present this award to you?" Bernie asked. By now, the realization of this honor coming to me was overwhelming. The first name that popped into my head was Walter Mirisch. "Great," he said, "Mirisch has great standing in the movie community. We would love him to be the presenter." When I asked Walter to present the award to me, he instantly agreed. Gosh, I was melting down fast.

Came the night of the awards, Walter made a great speech of introduction and said some wonderful things about me. I felt very humble indeed. Wellllllll, not so humble as to not want you to read a few excerpts.

I met Ralph Winters so long ago that when he first told me he had edited *Ben-Hur*, I naturally assumed he meant the silent version. The record book, however, shows we met in 1961 when I called on Ralph to work on a film we were making with Kirk Douglas.

115

The rest is, of course, history. The history of a long list of films we worked on together and the history of our friendship.

Ralph is a man of complete integrity in his work and in his life. He communicates well with producers, directors, and his fellow workers. He is open minded and completely flexible just as long as his Moviola is exactly forty-seven inches—no more, no less—from the ground; his light is set at exactly his hand level, and the pencil he works with is yellow—or else. Not too much for an assistant to remember, is it?

During the time I was making a few mistakes, Ralph did such pictures as *Front Page, Kotch, S.O.B., Victor/Victoria,* and *10.* While all his contemporaries grow older, Ralph remains perpetually young. By the way, have you seen the chariot race in *Ben-Hur* lately?

When Walter finished speaking, I got up to accept the award. My knees felt like rubber. I stood in front of all my loved ones, such beautiful people, and about a thousand other people. Editors, their wives, their sweethearts, their friends, my friends. Every one of them knew that there were four sprockets in a frame and sixteen frames in a foot. There was no way to fool them.

I thought about my dad. Even though I had never made it to become the head of MGM, as he thought I should, I knew he would be proud of me. I thought about Sam Zimbalist, and Danny Gray, and Frank Whitbeck, those great warriors from the golden moments of my beginnings.

My voice was a quaver as I told the audience about the eighteen-year-old boy who threw the film into the ash can. I asked them what they thought poor old Harry Reynolds, my first editor, would say if he saw me tonight. They roared with laughter. They loved it. I was a king once more.

Chapter 28

As I finish this book, I must again mention the names of some people who will be forever emblazoned in my mind and in my heart. People who helped shape my life and my career. I was fortunate indeed.

Margaret Booth had an aura about her. There was a uniqueness to her whole make-up. She waded through producers, directors, writers, film editors, and assistant film editors with knowledge and aplomb. She was usually right. Every time Margaret saw a cut she did not like, it was like a stab in her heart—and you had better run for the hills. But she was a good and true friend.

Blake Edwards. A man of tremendous talent. People talk of Peter Sellers who was brilliant as Clouseau, the fumbling French detective in the *Panther* pictures, but Blake Edwards created the character. He was definitely in a class by himself. When something would go wrong in the work, Blake would say, "Ralph, don't worry. Out of this adversity something better can come along." And, you know, it often did. In addition to all that, he was decent and considerate and lots of fun.

Walter Mirisch. Here is a man who came into my life twenty years after I had become an editor—but he came in with a bang. From the moment he walked into the cutting room with his sleeves rolled up to talk about censor cuts on *Town without Pity,* I liked him. Walter is a man of great sensitivity. Good common sense and great taste. There is a calmness about this man that sometimes drove me up the wall. But I am glad to say he is my friend and blood brother.

Sam Zimbalist. I can never say enough about this great man. However, I leave you with this. A friend of mine at MGM said to me one day, "Ralph, let me give you this scenario. You are cutting a picture for Zimbalist. You happen to be walking across a street. A car hits you and breaks one of your legs. Zimbalist hears about it and says, 'Gee, that's too bad. I wonder who I can get to cut that sequence.' Well, I never cared. He was still some kind of guy.

Last but not least: while this book is about my experiences and relationships in my beloved industry, I cannot end this book without saying a few words about a man who is not part of the industry, but he is a part of my heart. His name is Jerome S. (Jerry) Klein. He is about five-six or five-eight in height, but in my eye he is ten feet tall. He is my business counselor, the treasurer of my corporation, my personal advisor, but most important of all, he is my friend, and I love him.

When Jerry and I first met, I was already of retirement age and I didn't have two nickels to rub together. Well, maybe I did have just two nickels to rub together. He took me and my meager finances in hand, and within a year I was on my feet. When I wanted a new car, the answer was, "No. Your car is running. Drive it." And that's the way it went with many things. I could have killed him a couple of times, but I'm sure glad I did not. He has been a part of my life ever since. 'Nuff said!

EPILOGUE

In 1985, I lost my darling wife, Teddy. I was seventy-six years old. It never occurred to me that Teddy would go before me. I was completely devastated. It took me a long time to come back.

The following year, I found my schoolboy sweetheart, Lulu. She rescued me. She made me laugh and I fell in love again. We were married in 1987, at ages seventy-eight and seventy-four. Between us, we have five daughters, ten grandchildren, and two great-grandchildren. We manage to keep pretty busy.

I've enjoyed writing this book and jogging my memory back through seventy years of film joy and heartache. I hope you enjoyed reading it.

I may not have gone out with flags flying, riding on the crest of some gigantic Oscar winner, but my flags aren't furled, either. I still bother my agent, Larry Mirisch, regularly, and for the last ten years, whenever the phone rang, I've raced out of the barn like an old fire horse, ready to edit and consult.

So, fade out, slowly . . .

FILMOGRAPHY

Ada, MGM, 1961
Affairs of Martha, The, MGM, 1941
All-American Boy, The, Warner Bros., 1973
American Success Company, The, Columbia, 1979
Any Number Can Play, MGM, 1948
Avanti, United Artists, 1972
Ben-Hur, MGM, 1959
Big Trouble, Columbia, 1985
Boy's Ranch, MGM, 1946
Butterfield 8, MGM, 1960
Carey Treatment, The, MGM, 1972
Cry Havoc, MGM, 1942
Curse of the Pink Panther, MGM, 1983
Cutthroat Island, MGM/UA, 1995
Dime with a Halo, MGM, 1961
Dr. Gillespie's New Assistant, MGM, 1941
Executive Suite, MGM, 1953
Eyes in the Night, MGM, 1942
Fitzwilly, United Artists, 1967
Front Page, The, Universal, 1974
Gaily Gaily, United Artists, 1969
Gaslight, MGM, 1944
Great Race, The, Warner Brothers, 1965
Hawaiians, The, United Artists, 1970
High Society, MGM, 1956
Hills of Home, MGM, 1948
How to Succeed in Business, United Artists, 1967
Jail House Rock, MGM, 1957
Jupiter's Darling, MGM, 1955
Kid Glove Killer, MGM, 1942
Killer McCoy, MGM, 1947

King Kong, Paramount, 1976
King Solomon's Mines, MGM, 1950
Kiss Me Kate, MGM, 1953
Kotch, ABC Film Arm, 1971
Let's Get Harry, Tristar, 1986
Little Women, MGM, 1949
Love Me or Leave Me, MGM, 1955
Man on Fire, MGM, 1957
Man Who Loved Women, The, Columbia, 1983
Micki and Maude, Columbia, 1984
Moving, Warner Bros., 1988
Mr. and Mrs. North, MGM, 1941
Mr. Majestyk, United Artists, 1974
On the Town, MGM, 1948
Orca, Paramount, 1977
Our Vines Have Tender Grapes, MGM, 1944
Outfit, The, MGM, 1973
Party, The, United Artists, 1968
Penalty, The, MGM, 1941
People vs. Dr. Kildare, The, MGM, 1941
Pink Panther, The, United Artists, 1962
Quo Vadis, MGM, 1951
Romance of Rosy Ridge, The, MGM, 1947
S.O.B., Paramount, 1981
Seven Brides for Seven Brothers, MGM, 1954
Sheepman, The, MGM, 1958
Shot in the Dark, A, United Artists, 1964
Soldier in the Rain, Paramount, 1963
Spikes Gang, The, United Artists, 1974
Story of Three Loves, The, MGM, 1953
10, Orion, 1979
Thin Man Goes Home, The, MGM, 1944
Thomas Crown Affair, The, United Artists, 1968
Tribute to a Bad Man, MGM, 1956
Victor/Victoria, MGM, 1982
What Did You Do in the War, Daddy? United Artists, 1966
Young Bess, MGM, 1952
Young Ideas, MGM, 1943
Youngest Profession, The, MGM, 1944

Name Index

123

Movie Title Index